REA

Aston
Web G
w
Kai's Po
and I

# Astonishing Web Graphics with Kai's Power Tools and Plug-ins

David D. Busch

AP PROFESSIONAL

*AP PROFESSIONAL is a division of Academic Press*

San Diego    London    Boston
New York    Sydney    Tokyo    Toronto

This book is printed on acid-free paper. ∞

Copyright © 1999 by Academic Press

All brand names and product names mentioned in this book are trademarks or registered trademarks of their respective companies.

ACADEMIC PRESS
*A Division of Harcourt Brace & Company*
525 B Street, Suite 1900, San Diego, CA 92101-4495
http://www.apnet.com

ACADEMIC PRESS
24–28 Oval Road, London NW1 7DX
http://www.hbuk.co.uk/ap/

**Library of Congress Cataloging-in-Publication Data**
Busch, David D.
    Astonishing web graphics with Kai's powertools and plug-ins / David D. Busch.
       p.  cm.
    Includes index.
    ISBN 0-12-147615-4 (alk. paper). — ISBN 0-12-147616-2 (CD-ROM)
    1. Computer graphics. 2. Web sites—Design. 3. Kai's power
tools. 4. Plug-ins (Computer programs) I. Title.
T385.B865    1998
006.6'869—dc21

                     98-29445
                     CIP

Printed in the United States of America
98 99 00 01 02 IP 9 8 7 6 5 4 3 2 1

# Contents

# Preface

Instant beveled buttons! Images that dance off a Web page in fiery flames! Astonishing 3D effects! Eye-catching fractal textures! Glistening liquid droplets! High-tech chrome rules and frames! Webmasters always crave graphics effects like these to make their sites stand out from the crowd, but many don't know how easily they can be achieved using products like Kai's Power Tools and other Photoshop-compatible plug-ins. **Astonishing Web Graphics** *with Kai's Power Tools and Plug-Ins* focuses on creative ways to transform ordinary Web pages into triumphant prize-winners via inexpensive software add-ons and clever techniques.

If you've always wanted to know how to use all the features of Photoshop's built-in filters, but have been overwhelmed by the rich capabilities of Kai's Power Tools and other third-party add-ons, the answers you're looking for are here.

# Introduction

Most of the images you see on the Web have been processed extensively: cleaned up, sharpened, enhanced, or given a color tweak or two. Those eyecatching images that lure you into a Web site didn't happen by accident. Chances are, the designers of those pages knew a few clever graphics tricks that made their work stand out from the rest of the pack. It's also likely that you already have the tools you need to match those great images—all you lack is knowledge of how those tricks can be used. Virtually every serious owner of Photoshop also owns Kai's Power Tools plus more than a few other plug-ins such as Extensis's Photo Tools. The problem is sorting through the bewildering array of capabilities and options available.

If that description sounds familiar, this book is for you. **Astonishing Web Graphics** cuts right to the heart of some of the most misunderstood—but easily applied—tools in any serious Web worker's arsenal. You'll find surprisingly effective examples, simple-to-follow techniques, and tricks that serve as a jumping-off point to spark your own creativity into action. By concentrating on just one aspect of the vast Internet graphics realm, in the pages that follow we'll provide you with a meaty, informative look at a hot topic and effective category of Web tool.

All you need are this book, which includes dozens of color pages that showcase most of the techniques outlined, and the bundled CD-ROM, which includes working files, sample images, and finished Web backgrounds, buttons, rules, logos, and images. A copy of Adobe Photoshop and Kai's Power Tools would also be a good idea.

Your hardware ensemble doesn't matter. If you're happy with the performance of your graphics tools on your equipment, it doesn't matter whether you have a Power Macintosh or one of the latest G3 screamers, a plain-vanilla Pentium with Windows 95 or a dual Pentium II monster running Windows NT or Windows 98. Web graphics like those we'll be producing are generally small and lean, and won't tax your equipment or available RAM unduly.

Finally, I'm intending to extend the life of this book by supporting it with a Web site that includes other plug-in and Photoshop tips, royalty-free photographs you can use on your own pages, and other updates. You can access my page at *http://www.dbusch.com*. I'd also love to hear from you through e-mail at *astonish@dbusch.com*. If you have questions related to this book or have found a typo that should be fixed in the next edition, I guarantee you'll receive an answer from me (although it may take awhile if the missives pile up or I am traveling). I may not be able to help you with other thorny issues, but will try. I tend to avoid long exchanges with folks who demand to know why their computers lock up whenever they use Photoshop and their word processor at the same time, but I'm willing to commiserate even if I don't have all the answers.

Most of the chapters are free-standing; you can tackle them in any order you like. Here's an outline of what we'll cover in this book.

# ■ Chapter Outline

**Astonishing Web Graphics**

*with Kai's Power Tools and Plug-Ins*

1. **Plug-In Paradise:** Where we are going in the world of filter effects and how we'll get there.
2. **Five Minutes to Fabulous Effects:** Six astonishing effects you can create with the filters you already have—in five minutes or less.
3. **Your Filter Arsenal:** A roundup of the best plug-ins and the advantages of each, with examples of the effects you can achieve.
4. **Stunning Backgrounds:** Fast ways to create unique, seamless backgrounds using KPT Texture Explorer, Seamless Welder, and other plug-ins.
5. **Compelling Buttons:** Use KPT Spheroid Designer, KPT Glass Lens, and a few other slick tools to build efficient buttons that lure visitors to explore your site.
6. **Creating 3D Effects:** Make your Web graphics stand out from the crowd with these eye-catching 3D techniques.
7. **Rules and Other Web Artifacts:** Everything from KPT Gradient Designer to KPT Convolver can help build rules, frames, and other objects for a Web page that reinforce a visual theme.
8. **Using Filters with Text:** Create the typeface that launched a thousand hits, using some simple but effective techniques.

9. **Optimizing Web Graphics:** Filters for optimizing the color, converting to transparent or interleaved formats, and other streamlining tools.

10. **Designing Your Own Filters:** Every image editor has a custom filter facility, but most books gloss over using them. You don't need to be an imaging processing technician to create cool custom filters suitable for Web graphic production.

11. **Painting Plug-Ins:** Creating Web graphics from scratch or modifying existing images with filters like Xaos Tools' Paint Alchemy that simulate brush strokes and other artistic effects.

12. **Extensis Tools:** Using Extensis PhotoTools and other plug-ins.

13. **Effects Roundup:** A gallery of techniques and examples created with plug-ins from MetaCreations, Alien Skin, Extensis, Xaos Tools, Andromeda, and others.

    **Glossary**

    **About the CD**

chapter

# 1

# Plug-In Paradise

Say goodbye to learning how to methodically code HTML pages. That was last year, when mastering HTML from the ground up was the rage, especially after advanced, mind-numbing tools like cascading style sheets and dynamic HTML became available. Today, we have applications like NetObjects Fusion, Macromedia Dreamweaver, Microsoft FrontPage, and Adobe PageMill to do all that dirty work for us, including crafting eye-popping JavaScripts that float text and images around the screen as if they were alive.

This year, the single most important skill you can cultivate will be the ability to create alluring images that attract and hold visitors' attention, encourage exploration of a site, and deliver messages visually. You may be able to drag-and-drop your way to compelling layouts, but effective Web graphics still require solid techniques such as the ones in this book.

## ◼ In This Chapter

- Our Goal
- Why Plug-Ins?
- What Products Will We Cover?
- About You
- About Me
- How to Use This Book

# ■ Our Goal

Unlike general-purpose Photoshop or Kai's Power Tools books, we're not going to cram dozens of different approaches into this single volume. ***Astonishing Web Graphics*** takes the time to explore the use of filters and other plug-ins *specifically* as they can be used to create Web images. Concise, focused, and complete, this book should fill an important need, bypassing boring, basic tutorials in favor of sublimely useful how-to information with hundreds of examples and color illustrations.

In the very next chapter we'll leap into the fray with a clutch of stunning effects you can create in five minutes or less. A few breathless hours later, anyone working at a Mac or PC with this book will know

- How to create 3D type with shadows, cutouts, and perspective. Add a metallic sheen or a neon glow. You don't need expensive 3D software to achieve these effects. The same magic can be conjured inside Photoshop or another image editor using Kai's Power Tools and other plug-ins.
- Techniques for making prize-winning Web graphics out of images that aren't even good enough for the shoebox, using KPT's enhanced filters, or advanced plug-ins like those from Andromeda, Alien Skin Software, Extensis, and others.
- How to use plug-ins that bring off-color or dull originals to blazing life, ready for use in Web pages.
- The best ways to create impressive Web images from scratch. Even a photo intended for an HTML page may need some sort of object embedded in it, created with painting and drawing tools. You don't have to be an artist to turn out professional work. Image editing software today has some unusual filters, including Wind, which produces trailing streaks, and Lens Flare, which brings to the computer the image "defects" that lens designers hoped multicoating would eliminate.

# ■ Why Plug-Ins?

Why are filters so important for Web graphics? Plug-ins are low-cost (or free) miniprograms that insinuate themselves right into the Filters menu of compatible image editors for Windows or Macs and can twist, attenuate, and transform tired old images in exciting ways.

For example, through three iterations (and soon, a fourth) Kai's Power Tools has been a runaway best seller that has sparked the creativity of millions of users and spawned dozens of imitators. Although Photoshop 4.0 too sports almost 100 filters, and there were plenty of surprises in Photoshop 5.0, Adobe still can't touch many of the effects that KPT offers. MetaCreations' inexpensive KPT package is the absolute king of the hill when it comes to the breadth and richness of the effects you can create.

The most recent upgrade transforms this package into an integrated set of filter applications with superior controls and expanded real-time preview windows. Enhancements include Spheroid Designer— an incredible tool for creating 3D rounded buttons— and a revamped KPT Lens f/x tool (provides combinations of blur, noise, edge-finding, and smudging and is also great for making buttons.) The texture-melding Interform plug-in adds wild new effects to the redesigned toolkit.

Previous versions of the MetaCreations' flagship product scattered dialogless single-step filters and several applications like Texture Explorer throughout your Photoshop Filter submenus. KPT now collects everything under a single listing, which includes a Help entry. This book's readers will also want to snatch up KPT Actions, an inexpensive set of macros for Adobe Photoshop that use Kai's Power Tools to build incredible effects using multiple filters.

Other featured software add-ons will include Eye Candy 3.0, a great tool for creating beveled buttons, fiery images, or backgrounds with fur, smoke, or water drops; Xaos Tools' Paint Alchemy and Terrazzo, which add painterly textures and kaleidoscopic patterns to images; Extensis's PhotoTools, which can be invaluable for creating enhanced, graphical typefaces with a 3D flavor; as well as offerings from Andromeda and other vendors.

## ■ What Products Will We Cover?

This book concentrates on the version of Photoshop and Kai's Power Tools that most readers of this book will be using for the first year of the book's publication life: Photoshop 4.0 and 5.0 and Kai's Power Tools 3.0, and the corresponding versions of other plug-ins. By covering both Photoshop 4.0 and 5.0, you benefit in several ways. You get information tailored for the software you are currently using, when you can use it most. *Application years* and *Internet years* measure time on different scales. Major application updates arrive on a somewhat leisurely schedule; by the time this book is published, Photoshop 4.0 will be about 18 months old and Kai's Power Tools is nearly twice that. While high-end graphics professionals often switch over to the latest versions during the beta cycle, the transitional period for everybody else can be a year or more. As tempting as Photoshop 5.0 is, with its beefed-up Actions commands and revamped plug-in architecture, Photoshop 4.0 is far from dead.

In contrast, the Internet churns with new ideas and new techniques on a seemingly monthly basis. Holding back this book by three or four months to await the latest version of the major applications and utilities would have meant you'd lose a lot of valuable time in which this information could be helping you.

So, if you're a typical user rather than a bleeding-edge early adopter, this book is for you. You'll find the instructions here comfortable. Compulsive state-of-the-art enthusiasts will find that most of the techniques we cover do work just fine with the latest software, but that we haven't been able to comb through them—yet—with a fine-tooth comb reconciling the differences.

As I note shortly in *How to Use This Book*, if you use some other image editor that supports Photoshop-compatible plug-ins, you'll be able to apply the effects described. However, the specific menu commands and steps may be quite different.

## ■ About You

***Astonishing Web Graphics*** is for beginner-to-advanced Web builders who already know the basics of creating Web pages and who now want to spread their wings and learn more. It serves as a tutorial for experienced HTML authors who just lack graphics expertise, and an idea generator for Web veterans who want to spice up their work. Such individuals might include

- Home users who want to create personal Web pages using the hosting services of America Online or their ISP.
- Small business owners who need to build a site promoting a business and need to know more about using graphics.
- Corporate workers who may have Web page building in their job descriptions, who need to learn how to use graphics to beef up or help maintain their company's intranet or WWW site.
- Professional Webmaster with strong skills in programming (including Java, Javascript, HTML, and Perl) but little or no experience in manipulating or creating graphics.
- Adept graphic artists who already have impressive image editing talents with Photoshop or another application and want to learn how to apply their skills to Web pages.
- Trainers who need a nonthreatening textbook for classes in creating Web pages.

- Nascent Web page authors who aren't quite ready to get their feet wet, and want to learn more about what's involved before they jump in.

# ■ About Me

Who I am and what I've done are far less important to you than how I approach this topic. So, you'll want to know that I bring a photographer's eye to Web graphics. I'm a former commercial photographer who has written several thousand articles on photographic topics for magazines like *Petersen's PhotoGraphic, Professional Photographer,* and *The Rangefinder.*

That means I'm a nontechnoid graphics lover who turned to the darker side of technology (computers) in 1977 and have since written 56 books and a few thousand articles on computer and digital imaging. I've been a denizen of the on-line world since 1981. Back then, chat rooms could be found only on services like MicroNet (later CompuServe) and The Source, and the Internet was only a gleam in the eyes of science fiction writers and the shrewd individuals who actually made it happen. More recently, I've been building Web sites, writing Web graphics books like this one, and writing columns and features for magazines like *Internet World.*

So, I've been there, done that, and made my mistakes. Now I'm well-positioned to tell you how to learn from my goofs, and benefit from the cool tricks I've collected through the years. I'm not a computer science guru who approaches everything by examining paradigms, playing with Fast Fourier transforms for recreation, with a fondness for referring to pictures in terms of gamuts, rasterization, and adaptive palettes. For the last 20 years, I've been a user like yourself, eager to work with the latest tools and technology, and suffering from the same steep learning curves. Like you, I need to get things done and don't necessarily care if I understand how things work if I can do the job. So, I don't plan to teach you the theories behind internal combustion when all you want to do is get rolling on the World Wide Web highway.

# ■ How to Use This Book

Any author who must include an instruction manual on how to apply a book's lessons hasn't done his or her job. All you really need to know is that most of the chapters in this book don't depend heavily on the others, so you can turn to any section you want and begin applying the techniques you find immediately.

You'll need to know that you can use your own files to create any of the images and effects described. If you want to follow along exactly, you'll find the same files I worked with on the CD-ROM in folders named Chapter 1, Chapter 2, and so forth. There are additional images on the disk for further experimentation.

Owning a copy of Kai's Power Tools and an image editor like Photoshop, Corel Photo-Paint, or Photo Impact would be a good idea too. KPT works in the same way within any image editor that supports Photoshop-compatible plug-ins. For most of the other effects, we'll rely on the filters built right into Photoshop (you'll find similar filters in the other editors) so you don't need to purchase anything else. Several chapters will deal with other third-party filter packages, but they are optional for most techniques we'll cover.

Finally, you'll want to know that this book was written for those who already have a basic familiarity with Photoshop and Kai's Power Tools. In the step-by-step instructions, *not every step* will be described. If I tell you to apply the Gaussian Blur filter, I won't always spell out that you need to access the Filter menu in the Menu bar, select Blur, and then choose Gaussian Blur. In the beginning, I may use conventions like "use Filter | Blur | Gaussian Blur" to make things clear, but much of the time you'll be on your own for the obvious steps. Similarly, some filters won't function if you're unknowingly working on an empty transparent layer or haven't made a selection and that filter operates only on selections. Where I think a technique may need some clarification, I'll provide it, however.

## ■ Moving On

In the next chapter, we're going to jump right in and learn some great effects you can put right to work in five minutes or less. We'll stick to the basic filters included within Photoshop plus a few of Kai's Power Tools' easier-to-apply effects, so you won't get bogged down with learning an off-the-wall interface right off the bat. The instructions for the upcoming effects will be a bit more detailed. Let's get started.

chapter

# 2

# Five Minutes to Fabulous Effects

If you expected this chapter to ease you gently into the world of astonishing Web graphics with filters and plug-ins, you'd better take a deep breath. In 300 seconds—a paltry five minutes—I guarantee that you'll have a great-looking graphic ensconced on your computer screen. If you have another five minutes, you can create a second or third cool image. While there are three basic effects outlined in this chapter—embossed images, a gradient-filled button, and a glass lens sheen—you'll soon think of ways to adapt each of them in dozens of new ways. Each of the projects in this book should be a jumping-off point.

In this chapter you won't find any ancient history of the Internet, nor background on what filters are and how they work, or explanations of HTML. We're going to jump right in and deliver some examples of the kind of graphics you bought this book for. Fire up Photoshop or another image editor—you've wasted about 45 seconds of our five minutes reading this. If you have your heart set on background information, I promise to tuck some into later chapters in unobtrusive places.

## ■ In This Chapter

- Stamping Out Plaque
- Flip a Coin
- Click Here
- Adding a Halo

Note: As the last chapter said, you can use any image editor that can handle Photoshop-compatible plug-ins, but this chapter, like all others of this book, uses Photoshop for its step-by-step instructions and screen shots. Most third-party plug-ins, Kai's Power Tools in particular, operate exactly the same in Corel Photo-Paint, Ulead PhotoImpact, or similar products. You may find the filters in slightly different locations or use a built-in module with a slightly different name. However, most techniques in this book work even with non-Adobe products.

# ■ Stamping Out Plaque

You'll find quite a few metallic and 3D effects in this book, because they look so cool and add a techie look to any Web page. For our first project, we're going to create a realistic-looking engraved copper plaque, with raised lettering. I'll give you everything you need to reproduce the graphic shown in Color 1, including the original image. However, once you've learned the simple techniques involved, you can apply this effect to any image you like. You can stamp out gold, silver, or blue titanium plaques too with some slight modifications. To start this project, you'll need to copy the file Cathy01.pcx from the Chapter 1 folder on the CD-ROM bundled with this book. Then follow these steps:

1. Load Cathy01.pcx into your image editor. The original image looks like Figure 2-1; it's a grayscale profile of a young woman holding a flower. To save you a step, I've already converted the image into RGB color, although we won't actually colorize it until later.

2. Now, we'll enter some type. With Photoshop, you'll first want to press the D key to make sure the default foreground and background colors are black and white, respectively.

3. Using the type tool, key in the words *Plaques R Us*. I selected a Copperplate font, since the carved look of that typeface looks particularly good when represented as an engraving. Place a carriage return between each word, so they'll appear on separate lines.

4. Check the buttons that make the type align flush left. Use 32-point type, with 24 points of leading between lines; that will nestle the lines together snugly. Make sure the Anti-aliased checkbox is marked to smooth out the diagonal lines of the type. Click OK to add the type to your image.

5. Using the move tool, drag the type to the upper left corner to align it as you can see in Figure 2-2. You should be able to place the type so it fits in one corner of the image. If not (probably because the typeface you selected takes up more space at 32 points than Copperplate), you may need to use a smaller point size.

**Figure 2-1.** Original image

**Figure 2-2.** Text added

6. Photoshop users will now want to flatten the image, as the program created the type in its own separate layer.

7. The Emboss filter is the key to the engraved, 3D effect we'll end up with. Apply embossing to the entire image. Set the angle to 135 degrees, and set the amount of embossing to 150%. The "height" of the embossing should be set to 5 pixels. Your 3D plaque should now look like Figure 2-3.

8. Even though there is a pronounced raised effect, the plaque still looks flat and doesn't have a metallic sheen. That's easy enough to add with the Lighting Effects filter, found in the Filter | Render menu of Photoshop. Access the filter's dialog box and duplicate the settings you'll see in Figure 2-4.

9. Double-check and make sure you're using the Spotlight (from the Light type drop-down list); and have set Intensity to a value of 18 with Focus left at 0. In the Properties area, the Gloss and Material sliders should be moved to the far right, producing Shiny and Metallic effects, respectively. Ambience can be left at 11.

10. To add some extra texture to the image, choose Red as your texture channel (the color doesn't matter, since this is a monochrome image so far), then mark the "White is high" checkbox. Slide the Height control over to Mountainous to add a pronounced raised texture.

**Figure 2-3.** Embossed image

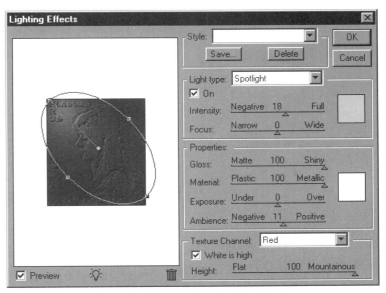

**Figure 2-4**. Texture from Lighting Effects

11. Move the light to the upper left corner, and adjust the lighting coverage by dragging on the handles around the perimeter of the coverage circle so that the illumination seems to come from that location, and is centered just behind the model's cheek. It will bathe most of the image by rotating the light—leaving only dark upper right and lower left corners.

12. Click on the light color swatch to the right of the Intensity slider, and select a yellow hue. The preview window should look like the one in Figure 2-4.

13. Optionally, you can type a name for this lighting effect into the Style field at the top of the dialog box, and click Save to store it on disk for later use. Otherwise, Click OK to apply the effect. You image should now look very plaquelike, as shown in Figure 2-5.

14. Now you need some color. Choose Image|Adjust|Hue/ Saturation. Check the Colorize box, then set the hue to a coppery value of 20 and saturation to 67. Click OK, and your copper plaque will be almost finished.

**Figure 2-5.** Finished plaque

15. Sharpen the image (Photoshop users should select the Filter|Sharpen plug-in) and save the image under a new name on your hard disk. You can see a full-color version of the finished project in Color 1.

# ■ Flip a Coin

A 3D coin would make a good complement to our plaque, and we can easily create one from scratch. You'll find this technique can be used to build a variety of disks and other shiny objects. We won't need to use an existing file, because the image editor has all the tools we need.

1. Use File|New to create an empty document. Make it an RGB file, measuring 400 x 400 pixels, with 72 dpi resolution. Photoshop users can check the Transparent button in the Contents area so the image will initially have no content. That will make some steps easier.

2. Create a perfect circle that occupies most of the image area. In Photoshop, use the oval marquee selection tool, and hold down Alt-Shift (if you're using Windows) or Option-Shift (if you're using a Macintosh) to constrain the tool to a perfect circle that grows from the center.

Note: From now on, I'll use the Alt/Option pair and Ctrl/Command duo to refer to sets of keys that have the same function in Windows and Mac OS. Mac users should not confuse the Windows Ctrl key with the Mac's Control key. The latter functions like a right-click in Windows, as PCs have two-button mice, and a Mac mouse has only a single button. If I mean for a Macintosh owner to press the Control key, I'll spell it out in full. If you see the letters Ctrl, we're talking about the Windows equivalent to Command.

3. Save the selection so we can reuse it later.

4. Select Edit | Fill and fill the selection with 50% gray. In the Contents area of the Fill dialog box, choose *Use 50% gray* and make sure the Preserve transparency box is unchecked. If it is, the selection (which is currently transparent) will not be filled in. Your object will look like Figure 2-6.

5. Now, you'll need to reduce the size of the selection so the periphery can be filled separately, producing an edge effect. In Photoshop, the easiest way to do this is by choosing Select | Modify | Contract, and use a value of 4 pixels to shrink the selection to a smaller circle.

6. You want to fill the area outside the selection, not the selection itself, so choose Select | Inverse next.

7. Press D to make sure the default colors are selected for the Foreground and Background.

**Figure 2-6.** A 50% gray circle

8. Now fill your outer edge of the disk using Edit | Fill. Choose Foreground Color as the fill, and in the Blending area of the dialog box; choose an Opacity of 80 percent. You want only the image that has already been colored to be affected, so check the Preserve Transparency box to protect the selection outside the disk.

9. Using the type tool, enter *Save $* as shown in Figure 2-7, using a point size that will nearly fill the coin. I used Copperplate again (so it would match the type in our plaque). Click the Center button, and position the type as shown.

10. Merge the type layer and disk layer using Layer | Merge Visible.

11. Now emboss as you did with the plaque completed earlier, by choosing Filter | Stylize | Emboss. Both the text and the darker rim around the disk will take on a raised appearance.

12. Apply Lighting Effects as you did with the plaque exercise, using the parameters shown in Figure 2-8. The chief difference from the last project is that the light source has been moved above the disk and is located farther outside the image area. When you're done, the disk will look very coinlike, as you can see in Figure 2-9.

13. We need to add a little glare, since this is a shiny coin. Use Filter | Render | Lens Flare. Drag the flare to the upper left corner of the disk, as shown in Figure 2-10. Select a brightness of about 61%,

**Figure 2-7.** Text added to the coin

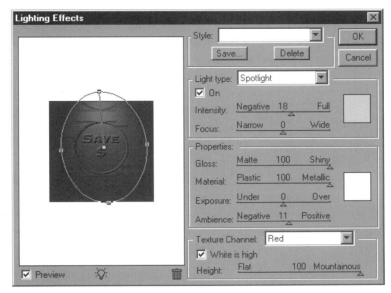

**Figure 2-8.** More Lighting Effects

**Figure 2-9.** Raised coin

and click in the 105 Prime radio button to produce a broad, bright flare effect. Click OK to apply the filter.

14. You must colorize the coin using Image|Adjust|Hue/Saturation. Click the Colorize checkbox, and use a golden hue of about 45 and a saturation of 45.

15. If you like, you can roughen the surface of the coin slightly, making it a little less mirror-like. Use Filter|Noise|Add Noise, and check off Gaussian, Monochromatic, and use a noise amount of 7. Your finished coin should look like Figure 2-11, and is shown in full color in Color 2.

16. To make this round object's surroundings transparent, so you'll be able to see the Web page's background, export the image as a transparent GIF. Use File|Export and select GIF89a Export. You can see how the image will appear by clicking the Preview box to produce the dialog box shown in Figure 2-12. While the image won't appear transparent in the preview, when the graphic is imported into a Web page the background will drop out.

A typical page using these two graphics might look like Figure 2-13. This one includes a gradient background created with KPT Gradient designer. You'll find more tricks for creating 3D graphics in Chapter 6.

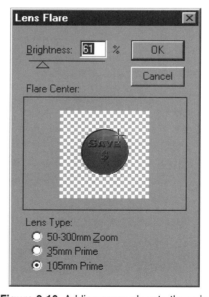

**Figure 2-10.** Adding some glare to the coin

**Figure 2-11.** Finished coin

**Figure 2-12.** Exporting the coin as a transparent GIF

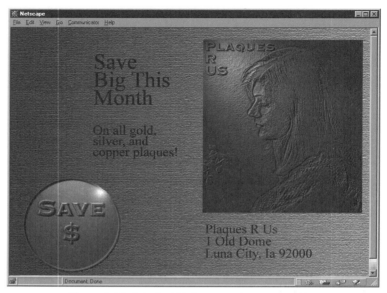

**Figure 2-13.** A typical Web page using our graphics

# ■ Click Here

Now it's time to give you a taste of what Kai's Power Tools can do.  Generally, KPT is a bit trickier to use than Photoshop's built-in filters, but you'll see that the effects you can create are worth the effort.

KPT makes it easy to build buttons that beg to be clicked.  KPT's Gradient Designer is much more flexible than the Gradient tool built into Photoshop, and the Glass Lens filter in Kai's PowerTools produces a shiny, 3D effect that turns simple ovals or spheres into shiny glass marbles that attract the visitor's eye and invite clicking.  I'll explain more about creating compelling buttons in Chapter 5, but this quick example should give you an idea of what's in store.  Just follow these steps:

1. Create an empty RGB image measuring 400 x 400 pixels.  Leave the background transparent.
2. Make an oval selection within it, large enough to almost fill the image, then fill the selection with the foreground color. (The actual color doesn't matter).

Note: Sometimes it makes sense to work with an image that's larger and has higher resolution image than you need for a finished graphic. You can play with the larger image until you get the effect you want and then reduce it to the actual size needed.  There are two advantages to working this way.  First, if you find the intended final size is too small to represent all the detail needed in the object, you can go back to the original size and modify the amount of reduction until you find a size that works.  Second, if you need to create multiple objects at different sizes (say, a large button and several smaller ones) and want to have them all look alike, it's easier to start with the bigger size, as scaling a small image up will always cost you some quality.

3.  Go to your Filter menu, Activate Kai's Power Tools, and select Gradient Designer.  A dialog box like the one shown in Figure 2-14 appears.

4.  Make the following settings, starting at the upper left corner in the Mode box.  Don't worry; I'll show you what to do:

- Click on the Mode box until Linear Blend appears.

- Click in the Loop box immediately beneath the Mode box, and hold down the mouse button. A menu will appear.  Make sure *Sawtooth A-B* is selected (a minus sign will appear to the left of it) and *No Distortion* is chosen in the bottom half of the menu.

- In the Repeat box immediately beneath the Loop box, click until the Info Area at the bottom of the Gradient Designer control panel says *Repeat 1 Time(s),* or slide the mouse to the left.

**Figure 2-14.** Gradient Designer control panel

- The Opacity box at the upper right has two kinds of controls, depending on how you click. Click and hold the mouse button until the menu appears, then drag down to make sure *Use Current Selection* is chosen. Then release the mouse button. Now click the Opacity box again and drag to the right until *Opacity: 100%* is shown in the Info Area at the bottom of the Gradient Designer control panel.
- Click on the Glue box and make sure Normal is selected.
- The Direction box shows the progression of a gradient. Move the control so it points at the lower right position, at roughly 5 o'clock on a clockface.

Note: KPT can be set in each tool's Preferences to return you to your last settings each time you access a tool. You can also press Ctrl/Command+E to return to that tool's defaults.

5. Move the mouse to the far left end of the Gradient Bar and click. The Gradient Color Picker shown in Figure 2-15 appears.
6. With the mouse button still depressed, move the cursor down to the color picker and choose a light purple color. As you move along the length of the color picker, all the hues of the rainbow are available. Moving up and down across its width changes the lightness/darkness of the color.

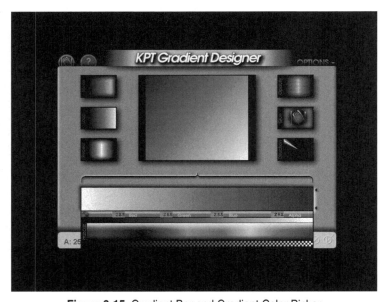

**Figure 2-15.** Gradient Bar and Gradient Color Picker

7. Release the mouse when you've defined a light purple for the far left end of the Gradient Bar.

8. Click at the far right of the Gradient Bar, hold down the mouse, and select a much darker version of the same purple. You can use the Red, Green, and Blue readouts that appear between the Gradient Bar and the Gradient Color Picker while you're holding down the mouse button.

9. Release the mouse button when you've defined a dark purple for the far right end of the Gradient Bar.

10. Look at the preview window, where the Linear Blend gradient will be shown. If you're satisfied with the colors, click the checkmark icon at the lower right of the control panel to apply the gradient to your oval selection.

11. Save the oval selection, as we'll be using it later on.

12. Now, invert the selection so the area outside the oval is selected. Fill it with the foreground color. (The color doesn't matter).

13. Access the Gradient Designer control panel one more time. Keep the same gradient values you just applied, but move the Direction pointer 180 degrees, so it is pointing at the upper left corner, at about 11 o'clock. Click the checkmark once more. Your image should look like Figure 2-16.

**Figure 2-16.** Oval and background with opposite gradients

14. Invert the selection again to select the gradient-filled oval once more.
15. Next, select the KPT Glass Lens filter. Its control panel box will look like Figure 2-17.
16. Make the following settings in the control panel. We'll assume you can figure your way around the panel, since each box is labeled.
    - Click the Mode area of the dialog box, and choose Bright.
    - Click the Glue box, and select Normal.
    - In the Opacity box, drag the cursor, if necessary, to set opacity to 100 percent.
    - In the Preview area, drag with the mouse to place the highlight in the upper left corner of the oval.
17. Now, click the green button at the lower right of the control panel to apply the Glass Lens filter. Your image should now look like Figure 2-18.
18. Now we need to make an oval depression in the center of the button. With the large oval still selected, make a copy of it, then paste down into a new layer. The copy will be the same size as the original oval.
19. Use Layer | Transform | Scale and reduce the size of the copy so it is about 35 to 40% of the width of the original.

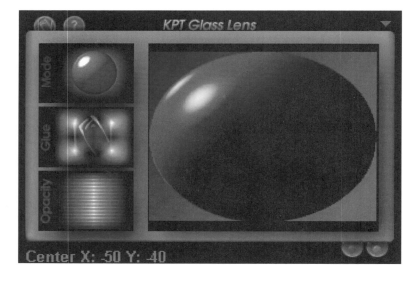

**Figure 2-17.** KPT Glass Lens filter

**Figure 2-18.** Glass Lens applied

20. Choose Layer | Transform | Rotate 180 degrees to flip the smaller oval around. Reversing the gradient in this way simulates the way light coming from the upper left corner would illuminate a depression, creating a vivid 3D effect you can see in Figure 2-19.

## Adding Text

We can add some text to the button to make sure visitors know they need to click it. I'll use a simple Click Here legend, but you can customize the button with a message of your choice.

1. Select a bright shade of yellow as the foreground color, plus a dark purple as the background color.
2. Using the Text tool, type Click Here. I used a thick, sans serif font in a 32-point size, separating the text onto two lines.
3. Center the text in the depressed portion of the button.
4. Swap the foreground and background colors. Photoshop users can press X to exchange them.
5. Using the Text tool, place another copy of your type on top of the first.
6. Reposition the text on the layers so the yellow version is underneath and to the right of the dark text. The image will now look like Figure 2-20.
7. Make sure the text, background, and button are all visible. Then flatten the image so the elements all reside on a single layer.

**Figure 2-19.** Depression added

**Figure 2-20.** Text finishes off the button.

# ■ Adding a Halo

If you like, you can load the selection I had you save earlier, and copy only the oval button to a new, transparent layer, and then export it as a transparent GIF. (There will be more on using GIF plug-ins later in the book).  However, if you want to use the button with the gradient, a light-colored halo produced in this exercise will make it stand out more, as in Figure 2-21.

1. Duplicate the layer containing the button and background, then make the duplicate layer active by clicking its name in the Layers palette.
2. Load the oval selection I asked you to save earlier. Press Ctrl/Command-X to cut the button from the layer, then press Ctrl-Command-V to paste the button down into a layer of its own.  You'll have three layers: one with the background and button, and separate layers for each.  Make the bottom (background/button) layer invisible.
3. Select the layer with the flattened button, then press Ctrl/Command-C to copy it, and Ctrl/Command-V to paste the duplicate down in a new layer (or use your image editor's duplicate layer command).
4. Use the Gaussian Blur filter, with a setting of 5 pixels, to blur the copy. Make sure the Preserve Transparency box is unchecked.

**Figure 2-21.** Button with halo

5. Next, choose a yellow foreground color, then check the Preserve Transparency box, and use Edit | Fill to fill the blurry oval with yellow.

6. Adjust the blurry halo so that it is in the layer underneath the button and is centered so it appears as a glow surrounding it.

7. Make the background we created in Step 2 visible, if necessary, and flatten the image. Your finished button and its background will look like Figure 2-21, and in its full-color glory like Color 3.

That's all you need to create several variations on one eye-catching button. We'll explore other button tricks later in the book.

## ◼ Moving On

In the next chapter, we'll take a look at the broad topic of what sort of things you can expect from Kai's Power Tools, Photoshop's built-in filters, and other plug-ins, with liberal examples. Consider the pages that follow an overview that details the amazing range of techniques you can squeeze out of one filter toolkit.

chapter

# 3

# Your Filter Arsenal

Plug-ins are potentially the most powerful tool in your Web image editing toolkit. They are capable of amazing feats of magic. Filters can apply a feathery layer of delicate brush strokes to a mediocre image and transform it into an Old Masters painting or impressionist masterpiece. They can reorganize the color palette of an image to create stunning—or garish—color variations.

Would you like liven your Web pages by blasting apart your image into a cascade of sparkling pixels? Or do you just want to add some subtle sharpness or contrast to make a low-resolution image that downloads quickly look good? Plug-ins can effect a complete make-over of all or parts of an image, or produce undetectable changes that make a good image even better. The power of image processing filters is that they are so versatile—and they've gained even more power in the latest Photoshop 5 release.

## ■ In This Chapter

- First Digital Darkrooms
- How Filters Work
- Filter Improvements in Photoshop 5
- Kinds of Filters
- What Vendors Don't Tell You about Using Filters
- Using Filters

This is the last chapter in the book that contains a significant amount of background material. All the rest concentrate on specific techniques and idea-sparking suggestions. However, I think that an overview of the available plug-ins and some details on how filters work can help you select and use these valuable tools more effectively. With a new version of Photoshop with updated filter capabilities freshly on the scene, a short nuts-and-bolts discussion is appropriate.

# ■ First Digital Darkrooms

Filters predate the Web itself to the very first "digital darkrooms" of the mid-1980s, including a pre-Photoshop application for the Macintosh called (not coincidentally) Digital Darkroom from a company called Silicon Beach. Back then, it was an amazing feat simply to create a computer that could display bit-mapped graphics at high speed, like the first Macs, and with the introduction of low-cost scanners (which in those days meant less than $5000) pixel-pushing applications gave many of us our first opportunity to perform on the computer the same image-enhancing techniques we'd practiced in "wet" darkrooms for so long. This new-found capability was so compelling that hordes of non-computer-oriented professionals, such as photographers and picture editors, purchased Macs specifically to use programs like the nascent Photoshop.

Filters were one of the most powerful features of digital image editors. They automated tasks that would be tedious or impossible to carry out manually: performing some sort of image processing on each and every pixel in an image or selection. They could, for example, compare each pixel with its neighbors to find areas in which there were rapid changes in density. (Most areas of an image have smooth gradations from one tone to another.) These changes could be considered "edges," and by increasing the differences even further, the edges would be made more obvious, and those features would appear "sharper." Imagine trying to do that manually! Figure 3-1 shows how sharpening/edge enhancement works.

The innovation that made filters especially useful was the first *plug-in architecture*. Instead of embedding filters deep in the bowels of an image editing application, programmers designed an interface that the image editor could use to pass information from the editing window to a separate software module, which could be plugged in and used as required. So, it was no longer necessary to rewrite an application to include an improved or totally new filter. Anyone who cared to could prepare a plug-in, not only giving early image editors a new degree of

**Figure 3-1.** At left, an image prior to sharpening.  At right, the same image with edge enhancement.

flexibility but prompting a healthy competition among programmers to outdo one another.

Although Adobe didn't originate plug-in architecture, inclusion of this feature in the first versions of Photoshop helped this image editor become the dominant product in its field on both Macintosh and Windows platforms.  Any image editor introduced in the last 10 years that hoped to survive, from MetaCreations Painter to Corel Photo-Paint, has included a Photoshop-compatible plug-in interface.

So, you can see that Photoshop-compatible plug-in filters are actually miniature programs in their own right, designed in such a way that they can be accessed from within an image editing application, to manipulate the pixels of a file that is open in the parent application.  Some plug-ins can load files—such as textures—on their own, too.

## ■ How Filters Work

Plug-ins are called filters because in the most general sense they function much like filters you're familiar with in the real world.  An air filter in your air conditioner and the oil filter in your car are designed as a sort of barrier that lets desirable elements—air or lubricating oil—pass through unimpeded, while things we want to keep out, such as dirt particles are left behind.  Filtering is a conversion process, converting dirty air or oil, say, into clean air or oil.

Plug-ins also filter, either by removing unwanted pixels and adding new ones, or by changing them in density or position. That's virtually everything that any filter does: deleting pixels, adding them, changing their darkness/lightness and color, or moving them around. Each filter consists of a list of rules, frequently in the form of a matrix, that tells the application how to modify a pixel based on the state of those surrounding it. Because filters affect pixels dynamically (e.g., the way one pixel has been changed can affect others when it's their turn to be processed), the process is often called convolution ("rolling together"). A typical filter matrix is shown in Figure 3-2.

A simple filter is the Invert plug-in found in all image editors. It looks at each pixel in turn and simply "flips" it to the exact opposite value. That is, a pure white or light gray pixel will be changed to pure black or dark gray. The color value of the pixel will be changed to the color opposite on the current Color Picker's color wheel. A dark blue pixel will become light yellow and so forth. This is the simplest kind of filtering possible, because the values being modified are already stored as numbers, from 0 to 255 for each of the three color channels, plus gray (assuming an RGB color gamut). A single mathematical algorithm can be applied to each pixel to produce the filtered image.

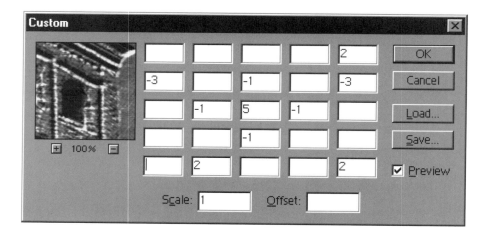

**Figure 3-2.** A convolution matrix determines how each pixel will be modified based on the value of its neighbors.

Other filters may remove pixels entirely or shift them around in an image in relation to others that remain in place.  The programs that make up filters can be very simple (so-called "one-step" filters like Sharpen or Blur), or extremely complex, bristling with dialog boxes, slider controls, buttons, preview windows, and other features, like those in Kai's Power Tools.

Image processing filters resemble photographic filters in some ways, too.  You can buy special effects filters to screw onto the front of a lens to provide wild diffraction, break an image into dozens of "bug's eye-view" elements, and even blur an image across the board—or only selectively at the edges.  Andromeda markets a line of filters with very similar effects.

While some features are part of Photoshop itself and are considered *native* effects, most are true programs with a life of their own.  Upgrading, adding, or removing a filter is as easy as deleting the old filter file and dragging a new one into the Plug-Ins folder of your application.  The next time you start Photoshop or another image editor, the application "builds" itself by looking for available modules, such as filters.  Any suitable plug-ins are added to the Filters or Acquire menus automatically.  One of the hooks built into the plug-in architecture tells the application where in the menu a filter should be placed, making it simple to classify filters by function or type.

Ironically, Photoshop's ability to use plug-ins has made it possible for other vendors to market products that compete with Adobe's flagship, but at the same time has helped Photoshop stave off the most serious contenders.  Entire mini-industries have flourished around Photoshop spin-offs. For example, MetaCreations' most successful product was Kai's Power Tools, but it has since become a conglomerate with dozens of related offerings, from MetaCreations Painter to KPT Bryce.  These add-ons made Photoshop even stronger in the marketplace, even though the program's rivals could accept the same plug-ins.  That's because these third-party enhancements improved Photoshop enough to eliminate much of the need to switch from Photoshop to another program to gain a feature here and there.

# ■ Filter Improvements in Photoshop 5

The most dramatic change in Adobe Photoshop 5—at least for fans of filters—is a whole new architecture that extends the power of filters even further.  This enhancement supports a new kind of module called Actions plug-ins.  For compatibility reasons, Adobe has retained the old kind of plug-in; you can still use your favorite Photoshop and third-party filters with no problems. Actions plug-ins, as you might expect, are kin of the Photoshop Actions macro capabilities introduced with Version 4. This new kind of plug-in can perform complex tasks that simply weren't possible with earlier filters.

Adobe's older plug-in architecture had some limitations, especially when it came to automating tasks with Actions. There were as many Photoshop functions that could *not* be included in an Action macro as there were those that *were* compatible, including most painting and selection tools. Now, with Photoshop 5, more tasks can be included in an Action, which improves the program's ability to apply complex filter techniques.

Another limitation was the filter's ability to operate only on a selection in the currently opened document. A filter couldn't affect anything outside that selection without some extra steps. In effect, Photoshop "exported" the selection to the filter, which was free to do whatever it wanted, and then export the selection back to Photoshop, which dropped it in the exact location occupied by the original selection.

An example will make this more clear. In Figure 3-3, a square selection has been made at left. Now, suppose you wanted to blur that selection, blending it into the surrounding area. By themselves, any of the blur filters couldn't do that unless you remembered to turn off Preserve Transparency.

**Figure 3-3.** Extending a filter's effect outside a selection requires extra steps

Those extras steps not only made Photoshop harder to work with, but created problems for third-party filter designers like Alien Skin, which wanted to make it easy to create buttons, edges, and other effects that extended "outside" the original selection.

Photoshop 5 now includes a new "socket" for plug-ins, which can accommodate more powerful add-ons. These plug-ins are all found in the Help menu or File | Automate menu. These include wizards to quickly resize images, create contact sheets, or change from one mode to another, depending on what mode an image is already in (e.g., change all 24-bit color images to Indexed Color, but leave grayscale images—which already contain just 256 tones—alone). Although the initial offerings are sparse, look for much more capable add-ons in the future.

# ■ Kinds of Filters

We'll explore individual filter packages available later in this book, but for now you might find it useful to have the different kinds of plug-ins categorized for you. Some of these classifications were created by Adobe or are commonly recognized. Others I've invented on my own as a way of organizing filters into logical groups.

## Acquire/Import/Export Modules

These add-ons have one thing in common: They help you load or acquire images for Photoshop to work on, or export images in a format compatible with other applications, particularly browsers (in the case of GIF and JPEG formats). Because they are plug-ins, these modules can be enhanced by Adobe or third-party developers, and then integrated smoothly with the image editor using the plug-in architecture.

The best example of this kind of add-on is the TWAIN image acquisition modules supplied with digital cameras and scanners. In olden times, a separate program was required to capture images from a scanner. These utilities were often separate image editing programs with support for specific scanners hard-wired into them, or modules that plugged into the operating system itself, such as the Desk Accessories used in early versions of the Macintosh System software.

Eventually, a consortium of hardware and software vendors got together and agreed on an applications programming interface (API) given the label TWAIN (reportedly for Technology Without An Interesting Name). An API is an intermediate level of software that hardware like scanners and digital cameras can "talk" to in an accepted way, passing along information like "Hi, I'm ready to roll" or "Here's a 24-bit image for you." An application like Photoshop, in turn, can address the hardware through the API, issuing commands like "Go ahead and down-load the image" or "Send image number two from the camera's memory."

With the API as an intermediary, Photoshop doesn't need to know anything about how the hardware works or what sort of commands it likes to receive. Nor does the hardware need to know how Photoshop operates. It's a bit like any situation in which someone who speaks, say, both Spanish and English must act as a translator between a Spanish-speaker and English-speaker who know nothing of the other's language.

## Production Filters

Production filters is my name for add-ons used in high-volume production environments to streamline color correction, density tweaking, and color separation. Alaras Tropix and Extensis Intellihance are filters in this category. Most of these are beyond the scope of this book. Most readers of this book prepare images for Web use, rather than offset reproduction, so we'll concentrate on Web techniques and the other varieties of plug-ins.

## Image Enhancement Filters

This broad group of plug-ins improves the appearance of images—sometimes dramatically—while not making major changes to their content. Sharpen Edges, Unsharp Mask, Dust & Scratches, and similar filters are all image enhancement plug-ins. Oddly enough, blur filters also enhance images; there are many images that can be improved by disguising defects with some blurring. This kind of filter can be applied to an entire image or to just a portion that you have selected. Figure 3.4 shows a typical image enhancement filter at work.

## Attenuating Filters

Photographers use the word *attenuating* to refer to things that alter a light source, e.g. "cookies" or "gobos" used to cast strategic shadows. Within Photoshop, this kind of filter acts like a piece of frosted glass, translucent scrap of canvas fabric, or grainy sheet of photographic film that adds texture to an image. These and dozens of other filters can be applied to a selection or a whole image, and operate in predictable, repeatable ways. Other attenuating filters include the various Noise filters and the Pixel f/x filters in Kai's Power Tools. Figure 3.5 shows an attenuating filter at work.

## Distortion Filters

There's a fine line separating distortion filters from the previous category, but the safest distinction is to note that these filters dramatically move pixels from one place in an image to another, providing mild to se-

**Figure 3-4.** Dust & Scratches image enhancement filter

**Figure 3-5.** Glass attenuating filter

vere distortion. Filters that map your image to a sphere, immerse it in a whirlpool, or pinch, ripple, twirl, or shear bits here and there can provide distortion to some or all of an image. The Vortex Tiling filter in Kai's Power Tools is a great example of a distortion filter. Figure 3.6 shows Vortex Tiling applied to an image.

## Pixelation Filters

Pixelation refers to a group of filters that add texture or surface changes, much like attenuating filters. However, attenuating filters apply their effects blindly without regard for the underlying pixels, while pixelation filters take into account the size, color, contrast, or other characteristics of the pixels underneath. This kind of filter includes Photoshop's own Crystallize, Color Halftone, Fragment, Mezzotint filters, Dry Brush, or Kai's Power Tools' Pixel f/x. The Pointillize or Facet filters, for example, don't simply overlay a particular texture—the appearance of each altered pixel incorporates the underlying image. Figure 3-7 shows a pixelation filter at work.

## Rendering Filters

Again, Adobe's terminology is a good way to describe filters that create something out of nothing. These filters may or may not use part of the underlying image in working their magic. Photoshop's Clouds filter creates random puffy clouds in the selected area, while Difference Clouds

**Figure 3-6.** Vortex tiling

**Figure 3-7** Pixelation filter

inverts part of the image to produce a similar effect.  Lens Flare and
Lighting Effects generate lighting out of thin air, while the latter also
applies texture to an image.  Photoshop 5's 3D Transform and Alien
Skin's Drop Shadow filters belong in this category, too.  The latter takes
the edges of your selection and creates a transparent drop shadow "behind" it.  The effects of a rendering filter are shown in Figure 3.8.

## Contrast-Enhancing Filters

Many filters operate on the differences in contrast that exist at the
boundary of two colors in an image.  By increasing the brightness of the
lighter color and decreasing the brightness of the darker color, the contrast is enhanced.  Since these boundaries mark some sort of edge in
the image, contrast-enhancing filters tend to make edges sharper.  The
effect is different from pure sharpening filters, which also use contrast
enhancement.  Filters in this category include all varieties of filters
with names like Find Edges, Glowing Edges, Accented Edges,  Poster
Edges, Ink Outlines, and even most Emboss and Bas Relief filters.  A
sample contrast-enhancing effect is shown in Figure 3.9.

## Other Filters

You'll find many more different add-ons that don't fit exactly into one of
the preceding categories, or that overlap several of them.  Xaos Tools'
Paint Alchemy is a kind of pixelation filter—but with so many options

**Figure 3.8.**   Rendering filter

for using varieties of brush strokes, it almost deserves a category of its own. Terrazzo, another plug-in from Xaos, creates repeating tile patterns from your selection and so is a distortion filter, but you can apply the patterns so they attenuate your image. KPT Convolver is a kind of "filter's filter," which is used to modify the behavior of other filters. We'll look at many different oddball filters throughout this book.

## ■ What Vendors Don't Tell You About Using Filters

Many commercial filter packages have an Installer or Setup program that finds or asks you where you store your plug-ins, and then decompresses the files in the correct location. Some filters, particularly shareware offerings, must be manually dragged to your Plugins (Photoshop 4) or Plug-Ins (Photoshop 5) folder. This is all pretty simple, right? Think again. If you accept the default installation routines, you're missing out on some valuable options—including the ability to organize your burgeoning filter collection in a reasonable manner.

In some cases, you're better off customizing your filter installations yourself. Here are some key points to keep in mind.

Use File | Preferences | Plug-Ins & Scratch disks to select your filter folder. It doesn't have to be named Plugins or Plug-Ins, and it can be lo-

**Figure 3-9.** Contrast-enhancing filter

cated anywhere, even on a network drive (although you should have the network drive mapped to a local drive letter, as Photoshop's change directory dialog box doesn't have a Network button). That means you can share the same set of filters with several compatible applications or even with more than one user over a network. You must exit the program and reload to begin accessing the filters in your new Plug-Ins folder.

Photoshop automatically hunts through any subfolders within the folder you have designated for storage of your plug-in filters, searching for any additional filters it can find. Therefore, you don't need to keep all your filters at the same folder level. My "main" filter folder is called Plug-Ins. Within it are additional folders labeled Filters (Photoshop's own filters) plus separate folders for Kai's Power Tools, Extensis filters, and a group of useful shareware filters.

Filters have the built-in capability to "tell" your application which menu they should appear in. Filters can be "installed" within existing Photoshop menus, although the trend has been away from that. For example, Kai's Power Tools' Diffuse More filter was deposited in Photoshop's Stylize menu in KPT 2.0, but starting with Version 3.0, the same capability can be found in the separate Filter|KPT menu. These locations can't easily be changed by the user (without fiddling with the filter code itself), and Photoshop will still place all the filters in their intended menu locations even if you've arranged them into subfolders.

If you have an odd application that doesn't search subfolders for additional filters, or you want to locate some filters on another hard disk, create a Shortcut (Windows) or an Alias (Macintosh) for the filter or filter folder and drag the shortcut/alias version into the application's main plug-ins folder. Most, including Photoshop, can find and load filters pointed to by shortcuts or aliases exactly as if they resided somewhere in the plugins folder. If you find that some filters work with one application but not with another, you can use this trick to create separate plug-in folders for each program, and include only the shortcuts/aliases for the filters that you know will work in each.

The About Plug-in option in the Apple menu or Windows Help menu will show you what filters have been loaded by Photoshop. You don't have to wend your way through nested menus to view this list.

## ■ Using Filters

I'll explain how to use particular filters in the upcoming chapters, but there are some general tips that pertain to nearly all filters that we'll be working with. To apply a filter, keep these tips in mind:

- Make sure the layer where you want to apply the filter is visible and active. A common mistake is to have a layer visible on the screen, but another layer is chosen as the active, editable layer. The filter you're applying will process the active layer, which may not be the one you want.

- Most filters won't work on selections or layers that are totally transparent (exceptions include Clouds and Difference Clouds). You may need to fill a selection with random noise, a fill, or something else so the filter will have something to operate on, even if the contents of the selection will be totally obliterated by the filter (as when you're applying the KPT Spheroid Designer and plan to make the spheroids totally opaque).

- Choose the portion of the image that the filter will be applied to, using any of the selection tools, including the marquee, lasso, magic wand, or one of Photoshop's specialized selection tools, such as Select | Color Range. Some techniques can be applied only to selections, usually because their effects extend beyond the original selection.

- Think about whether you want the filter applied to everything in the selection or just to the image area in the selection, then check or uncheck the Preserve Transparency button in the Layers palette.

For example, if you want to blur a selection so that it spreads into the surrounding area, you want Preserve Transparency off. Then, to apply another filter only to the blurred area (say, a texture), click Preserve Transparency again.

- It's often smart to copy the entire image to a duplicate layer (Duplicate Layer, from the Layer Palette's fly-out menu) and make your selection on a copy. You can play around with different filter effects without modifying your original image.

- If you don't select a portion of an image, the filter will be applied to the entire image. Since it can take anywhere from a few seconds to several minutes to apply a filter, you may want to work with a representative section of the image first before applying the filter to the whole thing.

- Don't forget about Photoshop's Quick Edit facility in the Acquire menu. It lets you load a small portion of a large image, so you can bring only the portion you'll be filtering into memory.

- Know whether you're using a single-step filter, which operates immediately (like Sharpen|Sharpen and Sharpen|Sharpen More). Others produce a dialog box with controls you'll need to set.

- Most filters also include a Preview window you can use to get an idea of what your filter will do when applied to a selected portion of an image. You'll find this useful to make broad changes in parameters, but I think it's still a good idea to select a somewhat larger area of an image and apply the filter to that on a duplicate layer.

- If you have a large selection, a complex filter, and a slow computer, find something to do. Even filters that work their magic in a minute or less seem terribly slow when you're sitting there staring at the screen. Filter experimentation may be all the impetus you need to upgrade to a Power Macintosh G3 or Pentium II system.

- Learn to use Photoshop's Fade Filter command (press Shift+Command/Ctrl-F) to modulate the amount that a filter affects your image, layer, or selection. You can dial in as much of an effect as you like.

- When the filter is finished, be careful not to do anything else (e.g., move the selection) until you've decided whether the effect is the one you want. This is especially true if you have a version of Photoshop prior to Version 5, with its more flexible Undo. That way, you can quickly Undo the filter and apply another rendition. You save your work often, of course, and are using a duplicate layer instead of your main image, but Undo is always quicker than Reverting to the last-saved version of a file.

- When you're really, really certain that the effect is what you want, save the file under another name (File | Save As... or use File | Save A Copy).  Then, and only then, flatten the layers to merge the effect with your main image.  Some day, you'll be glad you did save a copy of the file when you change your mind about being really, really certain.

# ■ Moving On

This concludes the generalized portion of our discussion, and it's time to get back to developing astonishing imagery you can apply to your Web pages.  In the next chapter, we'll explore techniques for creating good-looking backgrounds using filters and plug-ins.

chapter

# 4

# Stunning Backgrounds

For printed documents, anything other than a plain, white background is probably a bad idea. Web pages, on the other hand, gain much of their personality from the background you choose to apply. It's safe to say that behind every great Web page is a great background.

Backgrounds are certainly easy enough to apply. Simple HTML tags like BACKGROUND="myback.jpg" or BGCOLOR="blue" can replace a visitor's default background color with an image or color of your choice. However, too many beginning Web designers don't take advantage of all the tools available to them in building better backgrounds. In this chapter, we'll look at tricks with plug-ins that can help your backgrounds stand out.

## ■ In This Chapter

- Fast-Loading Backgrounds
- Background How-To
- Converting JPEG and GIF
- Additional Sizing tips
- More Backgrounds
- Creating Textured Backgrounds with KPT Texture Explorer
- KPT Textured Backgrounds

# ■ Fast-Loading Backgrounds

The first skill to master is the ability to create trim backgrounds that won't take an interminable amount of time to load. Plain colors are the fastest backgrounds for a browser to display, but images are much more interesting to look at. Background images can be in either JPEG or GIF format. JPEG can support photographic quality and 24-bit color at the cost of some sharpness when the images are compressed. GIF, on the other hand, uses lossless compression, but is capable of displaying no more than 256 different colors. In either case, if a background image is much larger than about 8K, some unpleasant things happen when a visitor arrives at your Web page.

Indeed, no period of time seems longer than the "ohnosecond," that stretch of eternity that elapses between the time a request for a Web page is initiated and the moment the first graphics or background actually appear on-screen. Unless visitors to your Web site have set some default background color other than gray, that's all they'll see until your own background or image is downloaded during those awful ohnoseconds. What's loaded when is more or less determined by the browser, but you can make your background appear more quickly with a judicious use of some plug-ins.

# ■ Background How-To

To see how plug-ins can improve the download speed of your backgrounds, we'll produce a quick example and then compare its size using various file format techniques. Follow these directions to see for yourself what a difference a few tweaks can make.

### Producing the Basic Background

We're first going to create a cloud background behind the iris, using Photoshop's native Clouds filter.

1. Load the file Iris.tif, located in the Chapter 4 folder on the CD-ROM packaged with this book. It's a 300 x 300-pixel file, which is probably much larger than you need for most backgrounds, but is large enough to be easy to use later to demonstrate the difference in file sizes.
2. Use the Magic Wand, with Tolerance set to 1, click in the white area surrounding the colored iris.
3. Choose Select | Inverse (or press Shift+Ctrl/Command+I) to invert the selection, so that only the iris itself is selected.

4. Copy the selection to a new layer. (Press Ctrl/Command+C and then Ctrl/Command+V.) Your iris will be surrounded by a transparent background, as shown in Figure 4-1.

5. Click in the eyeball icon at the left of the original background layer to make it invisible. You won't need it anymore unless you make an error and have to retrace your steps without the aid of Photoshop 5's History palette.

6. Create a new, empty, transparent layer by choosing Layer | New | Layer (or press Shift+Ctrl/Command+N).

7. Press D to make sure the Foreground/Background colors are set to the defaults, then choose a medium blue hue as the foreground from the Swatches palette.

8. Choose Filter | Render | Clouds to fill the layer you created with puffy white and blue clouds, as shown in Figure 4-2. The iris will be obscured at this point, but that lets us work on the clouds for several more steps.

## Producing a Seamless Tile

This 300 x 300-pixel background will not tile seamlessly, as each edge of the clouds won't match as they butt up against each other. Kai's Power Tools includes a filter called Seamless Welder that can produce images that tile invisibly. However, there is a second way of producing

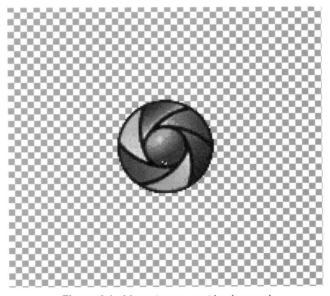

**Figure 4-1.** Iris on transparent background

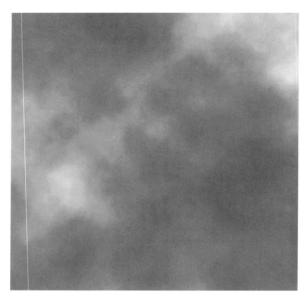

**Figure 4-2.** Puffy white clouds

a seamless tile that may be easier to master. The Offset plug-in can move the center of the image to each of the edges so that when they are tiled, four adjoining squares will line up to reproduce the original center. This confusing turn of events will become clearer if you try it out.

1. Choose Filter|Other|Offset, producing the Offset dialog box shown in Figure 4-3. Type in a value of 150 into the Horizontal and Vertical fields (so the image will be offset half its height and width of 300 pixels), and click the Wrap Around button. These settings will move the center of the image to the edges, and wrap it around so the entire tile is filled, as you can see in Figure 4-4.

2. You can see from Figure 4-4 that the clouds now don't match in the center of the tile. We can fix that easily. Choose the Rubber Stamp tool and the 45-pixel fuzzy brush.

3. Make sure Clone (aligned) is selected in the Rubber Stamp Options palette.

4. Click in each quadrant of the clouds and stamp over the center edges of the tile.

5. In the Layers palette, click on the name of the iris layer, and drag it upward so it is on top of the clouds layer. Note that the Offset filter has not been applied to the iris.

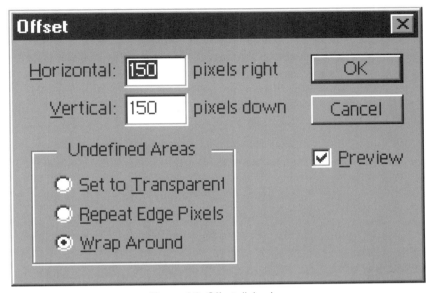

**Figure 4-3** Offset dialog box

**Figure 4-4.** Offset clouds

6. Make sure the iris layer is active; then apply the Offset filter to it, using the same settings as before. You'll end up with a seamless-tiling background like the one shown in Figure 4-5.

7. Choose Layer|Flatten Image to flatten the tile.

8. We've kept the contrast of this background high so you can see what it looks like more easily, but our tile has quite a bit more snap than you'd really want to see on your Web page. Use Image|Adjust|Brightness/Contrast, and move the contrast way down and the brightness way up. I used values of −80 for the contrast and +65 for brightness.

9. Use File|Save As and save this file as Irisback.tif, using the TIFF format. That will show you how much space the file takes up using the lossless TIF compression algorithm. Make sure LZW compression is selected in the dialog box as you save the file.

# ■ Converting to JPEG and GIF

Your Web page can use either GIF or JPEG files as a background. As you might expect from the discussion earlier in this chapter, GIF is a good choice for images that don't contain a lot of colors, but have a great deal of detail. JPEG might be your choice if you have many colors (e.g., with a smooth gradation) and don't need to preserve image information. (You probably won't want a highly detailed background, in any case.)

**Figure 4-5.** Offset background

We'll look at ways to save as JPEG and GIF with third-party plug-ins later on, but for now we'll use only Photoshop's built-in tools. Follow these steps to create some comparison files.

1. With Irisback.tif still loaded, use File | Save A Copy to store the file on your hard disk as a JPEG-format file (select JPEG from the drop-down Save As list in the dialog box.) Once you click on Save, the JPEG Options dialog box shown in Figure 4-6 pops up. Adjust the slider all the way to the right so that Quality: 10 and Maximum are shown in the Image Options area. Click OK to save the file.

2. Now, save the file again, using the same commands, only move the slider toward the left so Quality: and Medium are shown.

3. Save the file one more time, using Photoshop's File | Export | GIF 89a Export dialog box, shown in Figure 4-7. Select Adaptive Palette and 256 colors. You can also check the Interlaced box, which will allow the browser to load alternate lines (e.g. odd- or even-numbered) first, and then the remaining lines. An interlaced GIF may not load any faster as a background, but you'll find this option useful when creating buttons, rules, image maps, and other Web graphics.

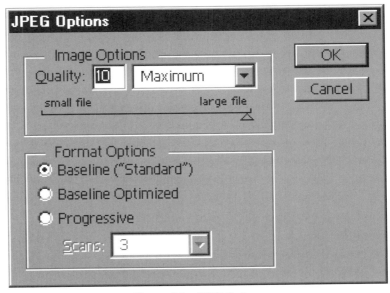

**Figure 4-6.** JPEG Options

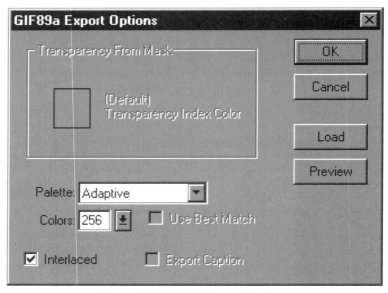

**Figure 4-7.** GIF 89a Export dialog box

## Results

If you compare the file sizes of the finished backgrounds, your results should be close to mine. The maximum-quality JPEG (using the 10 setting) and the 256-color GIF are the largest files at 27K and 23K, respectively. While you could use either of these as a background, you probably would want a more compact image for use as a background. Saving as a 32-color GIF cuts down the file size to 16K, but, unfortunately, produces the poorest color rendition. In this case, a better choice would be the JPEG at the 4 quality setting, which clocks in at only 9K. I'll show you a way to cut even this figure by an additional 25 percent—using only Photoshop's built-in tools—later in this section.

First, look at Figure 4-8, which compares the two different JPEG renditions we created. At its left is the background at the JPEG Quality level of 10, which produced the large 27K file that might take 30 seconds to download if a visitor had a slow modem. At the figure's right is the same background at the quality level of 4, which trimmed the image to a lithe 9K. Notice that there's a slight amount of image degradation, but the loss would be entirely acceptable in a background (or, for that matter, for most buttons or rules as well). Note: For these illustrations, I'm using the original versions of the images before they were displaced and faded, so you can see the image quality better. In Figure 4-9, you'll

**Color 1.** Embossing filters and Lighting Effects can produce a vivid 3D image like this one. Instructions for duplicating this image are shown in Chapter 2.

**Color 2.** A little lens flare give this coin a realistic metallic sheen.

**Color 3.** Radial gradients, KPT's Glass Lens filter, and a few other tricks combine to produce this 3D button.

**Color 4.** KPT's Vortex Tiling can generate some vivid, kaleidoscopic effects.

**Color 5.** The Find Edges filter adds a fine-art look to this photo of a Roman amphitheatre.

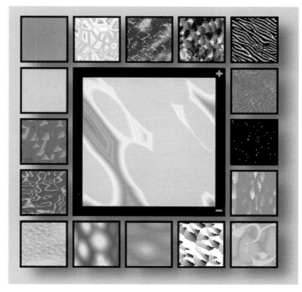

**Color 6.** KPT's Texture Explorer can create an endless variety of 2D textures.

**Color 7.** A button illuminated with two light sources, produced using KPT Spheroid Designer.

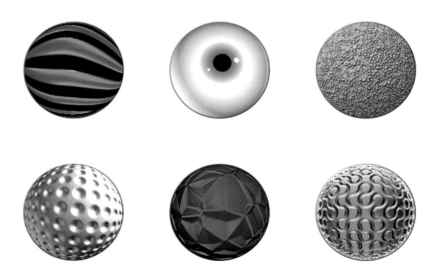

**Color 8.** KPT Spheroid Designer includes dazzling presets like these.

**Color 9.** Random swirls can be turned into eye-catching buttons with KPT Glass Lens and Twirl filters.

**Color 10.** Chapter 5 includes instructions for creating this 3D button.

**Color 11.** Believe it or not, these are all variations on the button in Color 10, produced using Emboss and texturizing filters like Craquelure (left), Sandstone (center), and Stained Glass (right).

**Color 12.** This etched nameplate has a 3D metallic effect, using a technique described in Chapter 5.

**Color 13.** Burnished metal effects like this bolt head are simple to achieve
if you know some lighting and texturing tricks.

**Color 14.** These buttons were produced using Extensis PhotoBevel.

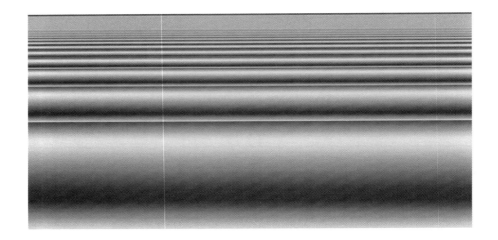

**Color 15.** A rolled-gold background can be created using Photoshop's built-in Copper gradient, followed by KPT's Planar Tiling plug-in.

**Color 16.** A single texture map, applied using different values of relief, can generate very different surface looks.

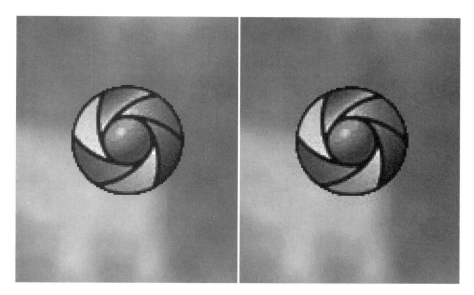

**Figure 4-8** Left: JPEG at Quality level 10,Right: at Quality level 4.

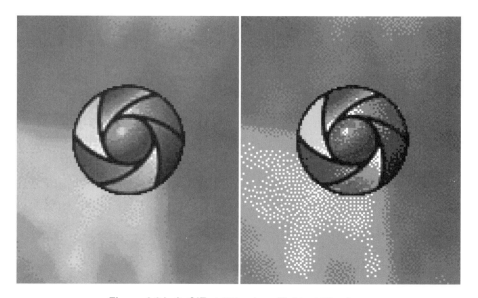

**Figure 4-9** Left: GIF at 256 colors, Right: at 32 colors.

find the two GIF files. By all means check out the original files on the CD-ROM bundled with this book to see the differences more clearly.

Even a quick glance shows that the 256-color GIF at Figure 4-9's left doesn't look nearly as good as the best JPEG image, even though its size, at 24K, is only a little smaller. Although it might not show up well on the printed page, the image degradation comes from an effect called banding when the original 16.7 million colors are reduced to 256. Instead of a smooth gradation, groups of similar colors are combined into bands. For many images, the fact that the GIF version may actually appear sharper (as in this case) won't make up for those lost colors. The banding becomes even worse when we reduce the colors to 32, as in the example at right. At 16K, it's almost twice as large as the 9K smallest JPEG, and, for a background, the additional sharpness is probably no advantage.

I created the smallest file of all—a compact 6K—by the simple expedient of cropping the background image so it fit into a 150 x 150-pixel rather than 300 x 300-pixel area. The lesson here is that you need to choose the best file format and compression scheme for your background, and the size of the tile is also important.

If you have many background files, buttons, or other objects to compress, you won't always have time to try out the different options we explored so far in this chapter. That's where plug-ins come to the rescue. HSV Color is one of the best of these tools for the Macintosh; for Windows workers, Ulead's SmartSaver is one of the most flexible and inexpensive options.

## Ulead's SmartSaver

This Windows-only plug-in for any Photoshop-compatible image editor is included free in PhotoImpact, but can be purchased separately from Ulead (http://www.ulead.com) or many other sources. It can help you generate backgrounds that download in a few seconds, even with slow modems. SmartSaver removes both the trial and error from the tedious task of optimizing GIF and JPEG files for the Web. Unlike the techniques used earlier in this chapter, this plug-in lets you interactively adjust image size and color palette and see a preview of your results.

SmartSaver uses a tabbed dialog box, shown in Figure 4-10, to streamline image conversion. As you've learned, GIF is a compression scheme that can technically be called lossless, because files are squeezed without eliminating any picture information. A GIF can be displayed by your browser with all the information of the original. However, the name is something of a misnomer if the image contained more than 256 colors or more colors than end up in the final GIF file. Be-

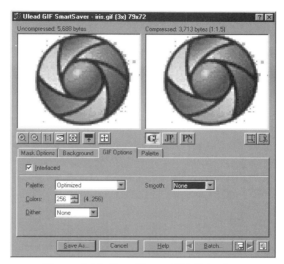

**Figure 4-10.** SmartSaver GIF dialog box

cause GIFs can display a maximum of 256 hues, some colors in full-color images must be sacrificed to represent the graphic in the GIF format. The colors removed can certainly be considered "lost."

However, because GIF nominally preserves all the detail in an image, the only way a utility like SmartSaver can further compress these files is to eliminate even more colors. GIF files may contain 128 colors, 64 colors, or even as few as 5 or 6. The trick to preserving as much quality as possible while discarding colors is to choose the right combination of tones. SmartSaver can create GIFs in which eliminated colors are represented by tones that are as close as possible to the original, or by placing colors so close to one another that the eye can blend them into an approximation of the original (called dithering). The hard part is choosing the best combinations of tones.

SmartSaver can also optimize JPEG files, but trims file size of these images by varying the compression ratio (which is where the quality loss comes in—more compression equals a degraded image).

JPEG files use a different dialog tab, shown in Figure 4-11. As I mentioned, for JPEGs, the compression ratio is modified. The number of colors remains the same in both instances, but the more highly compressed (smaller) JPEG version looks blurrier. If you're creating a background image with details that must remain clear or one with few colors, GIF is probably your best format for the job. If you want the background to include a full range of colors and can put up with a degraded image (and this is very likely to be the case—blurry or fuzzy

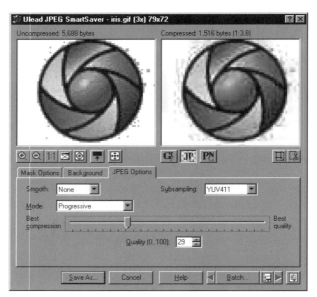

**Figure 4-11.** SmartSaver's JPEG dialog tab

backgrounds tend to be less obtrusive), then use JPEG. Tools like SmartSaver make it simple to interactively adjust file size, while monitoring the effects of your selections on the final graphic.

# ■ Additional Sizing Tips

As you just learned, you should use a background image file with the smallest dimensions you can get away with. A 128 x 128-pixel image might consume 18K, while the same image at 64 x 64 may be only 2.8K. Guess which one would download and display more quickly? The sharpness of background images isn't usually an issue. They're supposed to be unobtrusive, so a smaller graphic can easily do just as good a job, more quickly, if you're willing to sacrifice a tiny bit of quality for a more compact file.

If you don't have a tool like SmartSaver, save your background in both JPEG and GIF format, and use the smallest version that looks good on your page. While a 128 x 128-pixel test file was 18K as a GIF, it measured just 8K as a JPEG.

# ■ More Backgrounds

Here are several tricks you can use to enhance your backgrounds.

## Tiny Backgrounds

For the ultimate in tiny backgrounds, create a 5 x 1200-pixel file like
the one shown in Figure 4-12. We came up with a good-looking background that amounted to only 184 *bytes* (not kilobytes) and downloaded
in a flash. The 1200-pixel width ensures that the background will extend across even the widest browser window.

For this background, I applied a rainbow gradient created with KPT
Gradient Designer, using the multicolor technique described in Chapter
2. Note how the browser easily tiles it vertically to fill up the window
with multicolored stripes.

## Vertical Columns

Using gradients or dividing your page into vertical columns with your
background can add interest and provides imaginative formatting without the need for complicated frames or cascading style sheets. Try one
of these effects:

The 5 x 1200-pixel background in Figure 4-13 includes one column
in a contrasting color at the left side of the screen. Create a table with

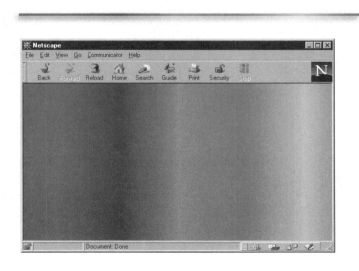

**Figure 4-12.**   Background using 5 x 1200-pixel graphic

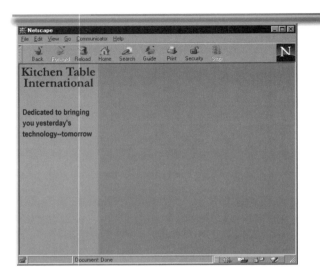

**Figure 4-13.** Columns in a contrasting color

a column the same width as your background column, and you can make columns of text flow through the background column. You can also add vertical rules and other effects, like those shown in Figure 4-14.

## Transparent and Seamless GIFs

Transparent GIFs (not all browsers support progressive JPEG or PNG files) make all the pixels surrounding the nonsquare object you want to highlight invisible. A single color (and only one) can be designated as invisible or transparent. While Photoshop is stuck with this limitation, Ulead's SmartSaver can convert multiple colors to a single tone that can then be rendered as transparent—a handy capability. When a browser displays such an image, it ignores that particular color anywhere it finds it and, instead, substitutes pixels representing the underlying background for the pixels of that color.

The background can be a background color or, alternatively, a background image that is tiled, if necessary, to cover a page's window in the browser. You probably know this. However, here's a technique you might not have considered.

Did you did know that you can use a *transparent* GIF as a background? The result is that a background *color* you specify will show through the image you've created as a background. Just remember to specify both in your HTML code, and save the background as a trans-

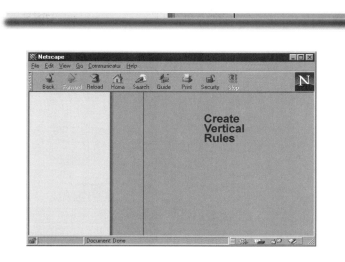

**Figure 4-14.** More columns in a contrasting color

parent GIF.  Figure 4-15 shows an example of a transparent GIF used
as a background.  All you need to do is specify a different background
color behind the characters in the logo for a whole new look.

## More on Tiling

As you learned earlier in this chapter, if you use more than solid colors
in your background, you'll want the graphic to tile seamlessly.  We used
one technique for creating a seamless tile with the Offset command.
However, in some cases, seamless tiling can be automatic, depending on
which plug-in filter you use.  For example, if you create a background
using Photoshop's Clouds or Texture filters in a 128 x 128-pixel size,
while the pattern may appear to be random, it actually will tile seamlessly.  KPT's Seamless Welder can also be used to create seamless tiles.

### 3D Backgrounds

Use a 3D background, and your text and images will appear to float
above a textured surface.  It's a great way to add depth to your page.
Any of your image editor's embossing or texturizing filters can add a 3D
effect.  Here's one way to do it. Just follow these steps to build your own
floating logo background, as shown in Figure 4-16.

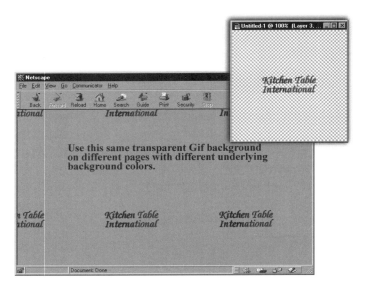

**Figure 4-15.** Transparent GIF used as background

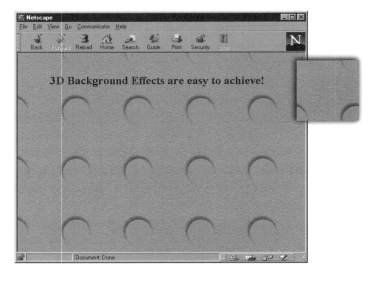

**Figure 4-16.** Glass attenuating filter

1. Create a background in 256 x 256-pixel size.
2. Fill with a more saturated version of the color you'd like to end up with. (We're going to fade the background when we're done.)
3. Add some random noise using your image editor's noise filter.
4. Apply a texture to the background. I used Sandstone. If your texturizer has a control for relief (the height the texture appears to be raised above the background), set it for a middle value. If you can control apparent direction of the light source, set it for top or upper left.
5. Add a logo or other graphic to a separate, transparent layer, then copy the graphic to the clipboard. I used a simple circle for my graphic. Yours can be type, an actual logo, or some other shape.
6. Blur the copy on the transparent layer, then fill it with black. (In Photoshop, make sure the Preserve Transparency box is unchecked when you blur, then checked when you fill with black.)
7. Paste down the original copy of the graphic, and move so it appears to have a blurry drop-shadow beneath it.
8. Use your editor's offset command to offset the image for seamless tiling. Touch up any center lines that appear.
9. Reduce the contrast and raise the brightness of the background, so it will appear faded.
10. Resize to 128 x 128 or 64 x 64 pixels, and save in JPEG format.

# ■ Creating Textured Backgrounds with Kai's Power Tools Texture Explorer

If you worked through the projects in this chapter, you've absorbed enough information on how to size backgrounds efficiently and create seamless tiles using the Offset filter. (You may also use Kai's Power Tools Seamless Welder if you wish.) Now we'll investigate one of Kai's Power Tools' most useful implements for creating backgrounds—Texture Explorer. You'll also learn a little more about the KPT interface than you picked up from Chapter 2. As you'll see, the KPT interface is quirky, but is very fast to use once you master it.

## Texture Explorer and the KPT Interface

It's apparent that Kai Krause doesn't care much for most user interfaces, which abound with labels you don't need after you've learned a control's functions, and confusing menus, controls, and options that distract you on the screen even when they're not available from within the program. Kai's interfaces, on the other hand, are a bit trickier to learn, but they share many elements, so once you've learned how a Power Tool works, you're a leg up on learning the next one. KPT Texture Explorer has a typical Kai interface, which you can see in Figure 4-17. The plug-in suite also has a second kind of interface, resembling a stop watch, which we'll look at later in the book.

When Texture Explorer loads, the rest of your screen is blacked out, and a preview of the effect you're going to apply to your image or selection is shown in the large preview window at the right side of the screen. Some elements common to most KPT plug-ins are shown in Figure 4-18.

**Kai Logo:** Passing the cursor over the Kai logo displays copyright information about KPT. Clicking on the logo removes the KPT interface and displays instead a larger preview of the effect you are working on. Press Esc or click the mouse to return to the KPT interface.

**Help Button:** This displays a terse but comprehensive description of the current plug in and how to use it.

**Options Menu:** This displays a list of options for the current plug-in and allows you to set preferences for that tool. You might find an option to change a tool's parameters to a default state. Under Preferences, you'll find a checkbox that, when marked, tells KPT to load the previous settings the next time the tool is accessed.

Settings can be saved on your hard disk for reuse later. In the center of the bar at the bottom of the screen, you'll find a downward-pointing triangle. The triangle activates the Presets menu, which can be a

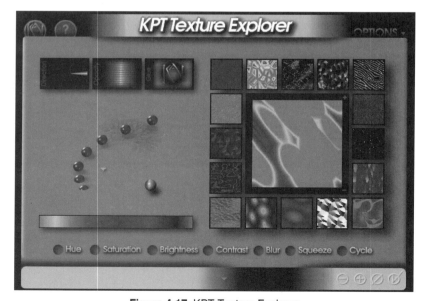

**Figure 4-17.** KPT Texture Explorer

list of presaved settings (as with KPT Interform) or a library of "swatches" that show samples of presets provided with Kai's Power Tools, or which you have saved during your own work. KPT Texture Explorer's Presets are shown in Figure 4-19.

If the library is a large one, you can scroll down through the selects just by dragging the mouse. There's no scroll bar; as the only things you can do in this window are select a swatch or move down through the list, Kai figures you don't need a special bar to activate the most logical feature. Click on one of the presets in the library, and it is applied to the center preview square in KPT. When you save your own presets, they are added to the end of the library. More common options, available from the bar at the bottom right of the plug-in, are shown in Figure 4-20.

The Add Preset button adds your current settings to that tool's preset library; Delete Preset removes those settings from the library. Cancel aborts your session in that plug-in. Apply transforms your image or selection using the current settings, and returns you to the main Photoshop window. Some KPT filters use a red and green button instead of the Cancel or Apply. You can also press Esc or Enter/Return to cancel or apply, respectively. Many KPT dialog boxes have control panels like the one shown in Figure 4-21.

The functions of these panels can vary. For example, not all KPT

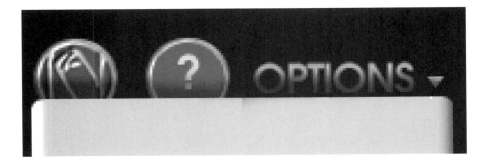

**Figure 4-18.** Common elements include (left to right) Kai Logo, Help button, and Options menu.

**Figure 4-19.** Texture Explorer presets

**Figure 4-20.** More common options, from left to right, are Delete Preset, Add Preset, Cancel, and Apply.

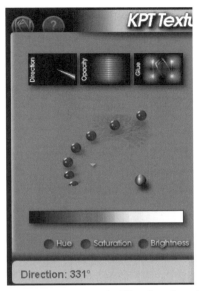

**Figure 4-21.** KPT Control panels for Direction, Opacity, and Glue

plug-ins have Direction panels, which control the orientation of the effect.  However, you'll usually find Opacity controls to set the amount of transparency for an effect, as well as a Glue control, which is used to define a merging method, such as Lighten, Darken, Subtract, Multiply, and Screen, much like Photoshop's modes.  Current settings for control panels are shown in the status bar at the bottom of the interface when the cursor passes over that panel.

The Opacity control is especially flexible, since you can drag the cursor to the left or right to set any amount of opacity from 0 to 100 percent, or drag it down to select a specialized Opacity mode.  These include the ability to apply transparency only to black or white tones, and to overlay the image with several backgrounds, including  zebra stripes and large and small checkerboards.

The textures created by Texture Explorer are based on variations produced by the mutation marbles and gradient band at the left of the screen.  These controls are shown in Figure 4-22.

Dragging across the top marble produces the most dramatic variations in the preview window.  Dragging the lower marbles generates the least mutation.  Texture Explorer can generate random effects based on panning, rotation, color, zooming, blending, and opacity, or just some of these. (Select which parameters to use from the menu that pops down when you click the downward-pointing triangle next to the

**Figure 4-22.** Mutation marbles and gradient band

mutation marbles.) Click the multicolored marble if you like the textures, but just want to see variations in color.

The gradient strip below the marbles shows the gradient currently being used to generate texture variations. Click the strip to see a popup menu of hundreds of different gradient variations you can use. You may also set gradients manually, as we did with Gradient Designer in Chapter 2. The gradient can be fine-tuned for the hue, saturation, brightness, contrast, amount of blur, squeezing (moving the center of the gradient from one location to another, while compressing the remaining tones into the space remaining), and cycling (moving the entire gradient). The buttons shown in Figure 4-23 are used to make these modifications.

Your generated texture effects are viewed in the preview windows shown in Figure 4-24. The large center square shows the current texture. The 16 surrounding squares show variations that Texture Explorer generates for you. These will change as you click the mutation marbles or change the gradient. When you see a texture you like, Alt/Option-click it to lock that texture in. Further mutations will affect only the remaining squares. Click one of the 16 squares to apply that texture to the center preview window.

**Figure 4-23.** Gradient modifiers

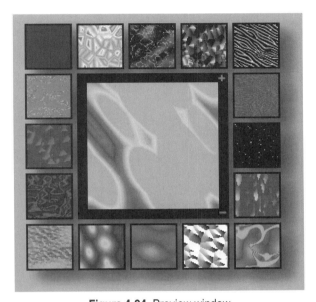

**Figure 4-24.** Preview window

If you want to keep a particular texture as a preset, click its preview; then click the Add Preset button at the lower right corner of the interface. A dialog box will pop up, and you can enter a name for your new texture.

# ■ KPT Textured Backgrounds

Here are some background effects that can serve as a jumping-off point for your own designs. You can see in Figure 4-25 that random textures work better than textures with strong lines and large objects. You'll get a better idea of my results by viewing the original color backgrounds on the file stored on the CD-ROM bundled with this book.

I created these four backgrounds, shown in Figure 4-26, in a minute or two each, using Photoshop's native filters. You'll find that many filters, applied to a 128 x 128-pixel image, automatically tile smoothly with no need to offset the image or blur the edges. The Clouds and Texturizer filters are two that work well.

The background at upper left was created by applying the Craquelure filter to a plain filled image. I used a crack spacing of 15, and crack depth of 6, and set the darkness of the cracks to 2, producing an interesting 3D effect.

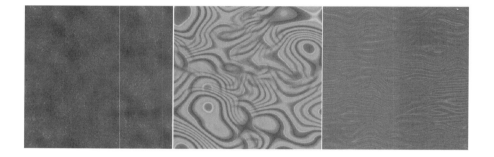

**Figure 4-25.** Textured Backgrounds

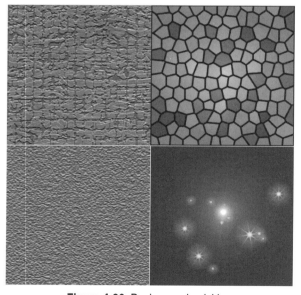

**Figure 4-26.** Background quickies

At upper right, the stained glass effect adds a dramatic look. In this case, the background doesn't tile seamlessly. Instead, each tile looks like a separate stained glass window and actually enhances the effect over a single broad expanse of segments filling the entire browser window.

At lower left, Photoshop's Texturizer filter, with the Relief slider moved to the 15 setting, produced a sandstone effect that makes the page appear to leap out. Brightness and contrast controls can be cranked down to produce a more faded look when you don't want this background to overpower your text.

At lower right, I applied the Lens Flare filter to a plain blue background, using the 105mm Lens setting. I used a large, 512 x 512-pixel background so the "sun" would be isolated in a broad expanse of deep blue sky. I finished off the image by applying Ulead's Particle filter, which is available separately from Ulead, or in the PhotoImpact suite. If you don't have that plug in, you can create additional suns using the Lens Flare filter, and then resize and place them on your image.

# ■ Moving On

Visitors to your Web site will explore more if you push the right buttons. You'll get some help in that direction in the next chapter, where you'll learn how to create interesting buttons using KPT Spheroid Designer, KPT Glass Lens, and other tools.

chapter

# 5

# Compelling Buttons

There's no getting around buttons—at least not without a well-placed click or two. The buttons on your Web page are the graphical equivalent of a highlighted hypertext link. Visitors are invited to click on a button or two in order to jump to another location on the same page, a different page on the same site, or a different Web site altogether. Unlike text links, buttons are objects that we intuitively want to click, because they resemble the controls on real-world devices, such as CD players and auto radios.

Buttons also can be used as a way of coordinating functions and tying like things together. Even without a text label, green buttons can mean "go" and red buttons "stop" just as a custom button you create can be used to indicate other options on your page. A certain kind of marbled button, for example, could mean "help" everywhere it appears on your Web page.

Buttons are most often ovals or rectangles, because that's what we're the most used to. However, in this chapter I'm going to show you how to create cool button effects in a variety of shapes.

## ■ In This Chapter

- Simple Round Buttons
- Advanced Buttons
- Button Variations
- Automating Production of Your Buttons

# ■ Simple Round Buttons

Oval or circular buttons look good on a page, especially when created as transparent GIFs that blend in with the rest of the background.  Here are some quick tricks for creating shiny or patterned oval buttons.  In each example, start with a 250 x 250-pixel empty, transparent document at 72 dpi.

## Shiny Ball

1. Create a perfect circle by holding down the Shift and Alt/Option keys while you drag with the oval marquee tool.
2. Click and Option/Alt-click on light and dark versions of the same color in the Swatches palette to make the foreground the light hue and the background the dark hue.
3. Choose the Radial Gradient tool from the toolbar (Photoshop 5) or specify Radial gradient in Gradient Options (Photoshop 4).
4. Drag with the Gradient tool from the upper left to the lower right corner, creating a shaded spherelike object, such as the one shown in Figure 5-1.
5. Activate the KPT Glass Lens filter, and press Ctrl/Command-E to revert to the tool's default values.
6. Click on the Mode control panel until Bright is selected.

**Figure 5-1.** Shaded sphere

7. If you'd like to move the highlight around to a different location on the button, drag it with the mouse in the Preview window.

8. Click the green button in the lower right corner to apply the effect. Your button should look like Figure 5-2. Creating buttons in this way is a basic technique you should remember for your own experimentation. We'll also use the same steps in some of the projects we'll discuss shortly.

## 3D Button

Create several duplicates of the button you just made, and try some of these effects to add a 3D texture:

1. In the KPT Spheroid Designer dialog box, press Ctrl/Command-E to return the tool to its defaults.

2. Click the downward pointing triangle next to the preview window at the lower right (see Figure 5-3) and select Caustics from the drop-down list.

3. A set of four cavities surrounds the preview at the center of the dialog box. Each one represents a different light source you can elect to apply to your button. Only the light source at lower left will be active. (It has a sphere inside it.) With this single light source, you can do the following things:

**Figure 5-2.** Glass button

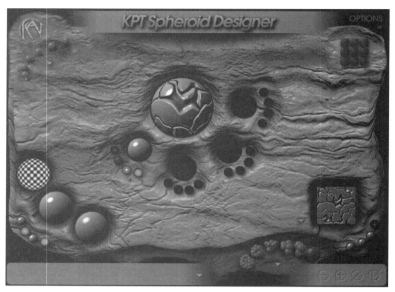

**Figure 5-3.** Spheroid Designer

- Click the small button at the right of the arc below the light source to produce a color wheel. Click on the wheel to set the color of the light.
- Moving in a clockwise direction, the next button can be dragged to change the light intensity.
- The next button around the clock controls the color of the light source that fills the shadows. You can leave it at black or select another color.
- The final button changes the "hardness" or "softness" of the light source by adding more or less diffusion, depending on how you drag the button.

Make any changes you like to the controls for this light source, and click the green button at lower right to apply the filter. Your results should look like Figure 5-4.

## Multiple Light Sources

To experiment with multiple light sources in Spheroid Designer, select another duplicate button, activate the KPT tool, and make these changes:

1. Don't press Ctrl/Command-E. Leave the settings as they were. If you've set KPT to automatically return to defaults between each use (in the Options menu), restore the settings used in the last project.

**Figure 5-4.** 3D button with Spheroid Designer

2. Click in the light source at the lower right corner of the preview window to turn it on. Note that the location of the light source controls has nothing to do with the direction the light will appear to be coming from. You can set that parameter separately.
3. Choose a contrasting color for the second light source. I used red to go with the gold of my first light.
4. Click on the original light source to turn it off. Then drag the highlight for the second source to the upper right corner of the preview window. Dragging in this way adjusts the direction of all the "on" light sources, so it was necessary to turn the other source off.
5. Turn the original light source on and click the green button. Your graphic should look like Figure 5-5. A color version is shown in the insert as Color 7.

## Variations

For variations, click the Preset menu at the bottom center of the dialog box, and select one of the choices from the library. Some examples of buttons I produced from these presets are shown in Figure 5-6.

You can also select the number of spheres that Spheroid Designer will create. For Figure 5-7, I clicked on the Make 1000 Spheroids button in the lower right corner. To spread out the tiny spheres over the button, I also applied Photoshop's Spherize filter.

**Figure 5-5.** Button with two light sources

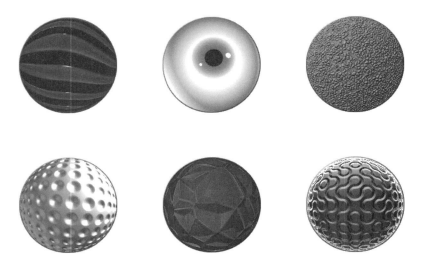

**Figure 5-6.** Preset combinations

**Figure 5-7.** Multiple spheres

## Quick Marbles

If you want to create a unique marble pattern for a button, that's easy, too. Try this:

1. Create an oval, fill it with a radial gradient in two shades of blue, and then airbrush some random yellow stripes on it, as shown in Figure 5-8.
2. Duplicate the graphic.
3. On one copy, apply the Distort:Ripples filter, set to a value of 300 to a selection that includes only the button itself and not the background.
4. On the other copy, apply the Distort:Twirl filter, set to an angle of 700, on the same button selection.
5. Apply the KPT Glass Lens filter to both.
6. You'll find these filters can leave a ragged edge. I used Select | Modify | Contract and reduced the size of the button selection by 10 pixels, then inverted the selection and removed everything outside the new, smaller selection. The finished buttons are shown in Figure 5-9, and in the color insert as Color 9.

**Figure 5-8.** Random stripes on oval button

**Figure 5-9.** Marbleized buttons

# ■ Advanced Buttons

Now you can apply some of the techniques you've learned to create even fancier buttons for your Web page. Work through the following projects to implement some professional-looking effects.

## Button with Raised Bezel

We're going to make a button with a raised bezel, resembling an indicator light. First, we'll generate a realistic-looking 3D bezel. Just follow these steps:

## Making the Button Bezel

1. Open an empty, transparent document measuring 250 x 250 pixels, and with a resolution of 72 dpi.
2. Choose the eliptical marquee tool, and click roughly in the center of the image.
3. While holding down the Shift and Alt/Option keys, drag a perfect circle that grows from the center point you clicked. Make the circle nearly fill the image.
4. Use Edit | Stroke, and set the line thickness to 16 pixels. Check the Center location button, and make sure the Preserve Transparency box is not marked. Click OK to create a 16-pixel circle.
5. With the Magic Wand, click in the stroked circle you just made to select it.
6. Use Select | Save Selection to save the selection.
7. Choose Select | Feather, and feather the selection by six pixels.
8. Press D to make sure the default colors (black and white) are active as the foreground and background.
9. Use Edit | Fill, and from the Contents drop-down list, choose 50% Gray. Click OK to fill the circle.
10. Choose Select | Load Selection and load the original circle you saved as a selection earlier.
11. Use Select | Inverse, or press Shift+Ctrl/Command+I to invert the selection.
12. Press Del to remove everything from the image except for the circle. This removes the periphery of the feathered area, providing a sharp edge.
13. Invert the selection again to select the circle.
14. Choose Image | Adjust | Levels to produce the dialog box shown in Figure 5-10.
15. Note that the tonal values are compressed into a very small area. Move the left (black) and right (white) sliders toward the center so

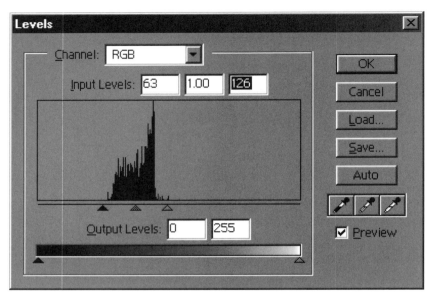

**Figure 5-10.** Levels dialog box

they mark off the area with density. Move the middle (gray) slider to the center of the histogram. Click OK, and you'll have a 3D "donut" like the one shown in Figure 5-11.

## Adding a Raised Button

Now we can fill the button ring with a raised button that begs to be clicked. Just follow these directions.

1. Using the Magic Wand, click inside the button ring to select it.
2. Choose the Radial Gradient tool from the toolbar (if you're using Photoshop 5), or select the Gradient tool, then choose Radial from the Gradient Options palette if you're using Photoshop 4.
3. In the Swatches palette, click on a bright red to make it the foreground, and Alt/Option click on a very dark red to make it the background color.
4. Apply the gradient to the circular selection, dragging from the upper left to the lower right.
5. Activate the KPT Glass Lens filter. Press Ctrl/Command-E to return the plug-in's settings to the default.
6. Click the Mode control panel to set the mode to Bright. Then click the green Apply button to process your button with the Glass Lens filter. Your button should now look like the one in Figure 5-12 and in the color insert as Color 10.

**Figure 5-11.** Raised donut

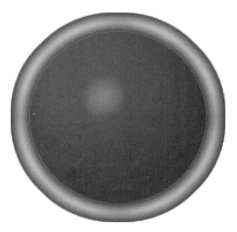

**Figure 5-12.** Finished button

# ■ Button Variations

One of the coolest things about plug-ins is that they can transform any basic object into something completely new with little effort. It took us quite a few steps to produce the basic beveled button. Now I'm going to show you several variations using nothing more than plug-ins.

### Thumbtack Button

1. Duplicate the button you just made.
2. Load the selection for the bevel.
3. Apply the KPT Glass Lens filter to the selection.
4. Use Filter|Fade (or press Shift+Ctrl/Command+F) and fade the effects of the KPT filter by about 50 percent.
5. Use Adjust|Brightness/Contrast to increase brightness by +15, and contrast by +25. (You may need to use different settings to get an effect you like.) Your button will end up like the one shown in Figure 5-13.

### Inverted Pie Plate

1. Make another duplicate of your original button.
2. Apply the Filter|Stylize|Emboss filter to generate a new variation.

**Figure 5-13.** Thumbtack button

3. Use the Rubber Stamp tool to fill in the "depression" that's located where the original button had a highlight.

4. Use Image | Adjust | Hue/Saturation to add color to the button. Click the Colorize box, set Saturation to a value that looks good (I used 25%), and choose the color you want for the button from the Hue slider. Your variation should look like the one shown in Figure 5-14.

## Multibuttons

1. Make a duplicate of the embossed button you just created.
2. Using the duplicate, load the outer-circle selection.
3. Inverse the selection.
4. On the duplicate apply the Texture | Mosaic Tiles filter.
5. Create two more duplicates of the original embossed button.
6. Repeat steps 2 and 3. Then apply the Texture | Texturizer filter, using Sandstone as the texture for one button.
7. Try again, applying the Texture | Stained Glass filter, followed by Stylize | Emboss. Fade the Emboss filter to about 40%.

If you follow all these steps, you'll end up with buttons like the ones shown in Figure 5-15.

**Figure 5-14.** Inverted pie plate

**Figure 5-15.** Button variations

## Rectangular Buttons

Here are some more rectangular buttons you can create with a few plug-ins.  Just follow these steps:

1. Create an empty, 250 x 250 pixel transparent document at 72 dpi, as before.
2. Select a rectangular area.
3. Choose the Linear Gradient Tool (specify Linear from the toolbox with Photoshop 5, or using the Gradient Options palette in Photoshop 4.)
4. In the Gradient Options palette, use the pull-down Gradient list and select Copper.
5. Holding down the Shift key, drag from the top to the bottom of the selection to add a coppery sheen.
6. Make two duplicates of the image, and apply the Distort | Glass filter, set to Frosted, to one of them, and the Texture | Texturizer filter at its Canvas setting to the other.  You'll end up with three basic buttons like the ones shown in Figure 5-16.

If you'd rather have  gold, silver, or some other color metal, just use the Image | Adjust | Hue/Saturation dialog box and adjust hue to get the exact sheen you want.

Of course, these three buttons look a little "flat" despite the coppery tone. You can add a raised bezel using one of the techniques that follow, or use plug-ins designed specifically for making buttons.  We'll look at a couple later in this chapter, too.

**Figure 5-16.** Three coppery buttons

## Steel Yourself and Test Your Metal

Shiny metallic effects look good on Web pages when a high-tech image is desired.  The key to successful heavy metal buttons is to produce realistic reflections and surface textures, similar to what you might see on a copper plaque, polished mirror, or etching.  Here are three quick ways of getting steel, silver, or gold effects for your Web graphics.

Figure 5-17 and Color 12 show a metallic etched nameplate, like one you might see on the door of an executive, or maybe an executive washroom.  You can duplicate it by following these steps:

1. In an empty, transparent document, create a rectangular selection.
2. Apply a light-gold to dark-gold radial gradient diagonally.
3. Texturize the surface using the Glass filter, as we just did with the copper button.
4. Next, use the Image|Adjust|Posterize (set to 12 levels) to introduce banding—simulating the highlights you might get on a nameplate like this.
5. Make three copies of the nameplate.  Lighten one, darken the second, and leave the third alone.
6. Offset the copies slightly, moving the lightened version to the top edge, the darkened version to the bottom edge, and stacking

**Figure 5-17.**Etched nameplate

the unaltered nameplate on top of the other two using Photoshop's Layers.

7. If you want etched text like my example, create the text, then repeat
Step 5, but stack the dark version at top, light version at the bottom, and normal text on top of all of them. The text appears to
be sunk into the metallic surface.

8. As a final touch, I created four 3D rivets, filling them with the same radial blur, and then added extra contrast to make them seem to
pop out from the nameplate.

## Steel Bolt

Next, we'll create a satin-finished square bolt used as an industrial-
strength button.  Just follow these steps to create your own version.

1. Create a square button, approximately 250 x 250 pixels.

2. Using KPT Gradient Designer or Photoshop's own Gradient Options editing option, create a linear gradient using four different shades of
gray: medium dark to light gray to medium gray to very dark
gray.

3. Apply the gradient diagonally to the button by dragging from upper left
to lower right.

4. Use Image | Canvas Size and type in 300 pixels for both the width and height. The button will enlarge so that it has a 50-pixel border around it.

5. With the Magic Wand, select the border. Then apply the same gradient vertically, dragging from the top to the bottom.

6. With the border still selected, apply the Noise | Add Noise filter, with the Amount set to 13 and the Monochromatic button checked.

7. Invert the selection, and apply noise to the center of the button, with the Amount set to 17.

8. Now, we're going to use the dark/medium/light trick we just applied to create grooves in the button. Select a thin horizontal section from the center of the button, and paste it down three times. Darken one, lighten the second, and leave the third as it is.

9. Make the button layer visible, so that only the horizontal groove is visible. Choose Layer | Merge Visible to combine all three layers of the groove.

10. Copy the groove and paste down into a new layer.

11. Choose Layer | Transform | Rotate 90 degrees CC (if you're using Photoshop 4) or the same transform selection from the Edit menu (if you're using Photoshop 5).

12. Select the center part of the vertical groove and delete it, leaving a finished horizontal/vertical groove like that shown in Figure 5-18. The finished bolt can be seen in Figure 5-19 and in the color insert as Color 13.

# ■ Automating Production of Your Buttons

Several tools are available to automate production of buttons. Alien Skin's Eye Candy, Ulead Button Designer (available as a separate product in WebRazor, but furnished free in PhotoImpact), and Extensis's PhotoTools PhotoBevel are among the best for creating raised, 3D buttons. In this section, I'll show you how each of them works.

In all cases, I'll work with a rectangular button that has been filled with a light yellow/dark yellow linear gradient from the upper left corner to the lower right corner.

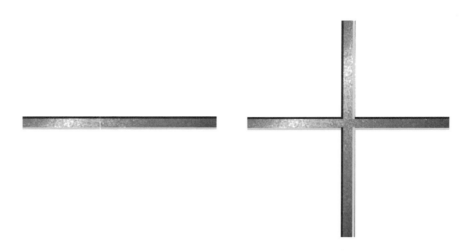

**Figure 5-18.** Stacked grooves

**Figure 5-19.** Finished bolt

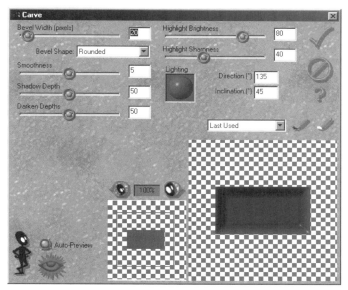

**Figure 5-20.** Eye Candy Carve dialog box

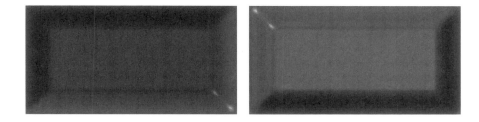

**Figure 5-21.** Eye Candy Carve and Inner Bevel effects

## Alien Skin Eye Candy

Alien Skin's Eye Candy features several plug-ins that make realistic bevels. All use similar dialog boxes, like the one in Figure 5-20. In each case, you can control the bevel width, depth, smoothness, shadows, lighting qualities, and other parameters. Variations can produce carved, raised, or other effects. Figure 5-21 shows some of the possibilities.

## Extensis PhotoTools

PhotoTools' PhotoBevel has an incredible array of variations, and lets you create double bevels, sloped sides, or other effects. The tool's dialog box is shown in Figure 5-22, and three examples in Figure 5-23.

PhotoTools also includes PhotoButton, which was especially designed for creating buttons for Web pages. Lighting, bevel size and shape, and dozens of other parameters can be specified using this flexible tool.

## Ulead Buttonizer

Ulead's button designer filters are among the most versatile we've seen. They allow you to create good-looking Web buttons from any shape.

The Buttonizer (Any Shape) allows you to take a selection and turn it into a button-like image. You can use the boundaries of your selection

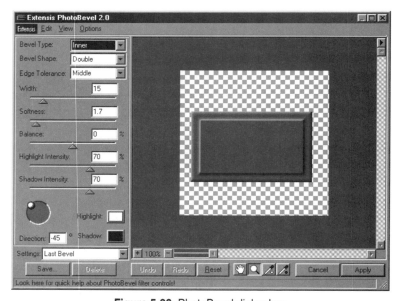

**Figure 5-22.** PhotoBevel dialog box

as the outer limits for the final button size, grow the button around the boundaries or inside them, adjust elevation and lateral position of the light source, or specify recessed buttons. Buttonizer's dialog box is shown in Figure 5-24.

# ■ Moving On

We're finished with button techniques for now, but will touch on this topic frequently in the coming chapters, especially those that deal with 3D effects and rules. In fact, 3D is the topic of the very next chapter.

**Figure 5-23.** PhotoBevel effects

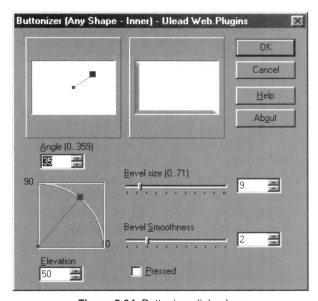

**Figure 5-24.** Buttonizer dialog box

chapter

# 6

# Creating 3D Effects

Some of the most stunning effects you can create for your Web page involve ersatz 3D images. The idea is to create *not* a real-world object that your visitor can touch, but an image so realistic that it touches your visitor in some way. Although you may end up with flat, 2D images on a printed page, the ability to provide perspective adds. . . can we say it?. . . an extra dimension to your work.

Although we've already experimented with 3D effects in this book, this chapter will concentrate on some easy techniques you can use to create buttons, rules, and type that seems to leap out from the page.

## ■ In This Chapter

- What Is 3D Rendering?
- Textures
- Drop Shadows
- Automating Shadows
- Instant Bevels

## ■ What Is 3D Rendering?

To take your Web pages into the third dimension, it helps to start in the 2D world. If you think about ancient Egyptian tomb drawings, you can understand just how flat two-dimensional representations can be. They have only height and width, with no depth at all. It's difficult to represent real-world objects in this way. The Egyptians frequently drew all human figures with their faces in profile because profiles were easier to sketch.

Moreover, in 2D drawings, every object exists in the same imaginary plane. You can't just draw something that is farther away in a smaller size; there's no way the viewer can tell if the half-size human, for example, is farther away or simply a smaller person. A 2D drawing lacks the perspective that three dimensions give us.

When we view things in real life, we can perceive depth because we use two eyes to view the scene, each eye having a slightly different point of view. Our brain "knows" that when an object looks almost identical through either eye, it must be farther away, because the relative differences as seen through viewpoints only a few inches apart are small. When an object is very close to our eyes, those scant inches present the brain with significantly different views of the object, so we know it is "close." That's how depth perception works and why we see things in 3D.

A Web page, on the other hand, is a flat representation of a scene. Everything on the page is the exact distance away from our eyes. Unless your Web page includes VRML objects, which require special viewers or browsers, it's impossible to produce a true 3D image unless we can give each eye a different view, as is done with 3D pictures and holograms. However, we can represent depth by including the visual cues that our brain has learned represent distance.

For example, objects appear to get smaller as the distance grows between them and our eyes. If we see two men in a photograph, and one appears one-sixth the height of the other, our brain assumes that they are roughly the same size, and that one is farther away. A single object that extends a great distance into a background, such as a stone wall, will recede or get smaller along its length.

Figure 6-1 shows two pairs of buttons. We see each of the buttons as a rounded, 3D object, because they have shading and highlights that tell our eyes we're looking at something raised above the surface. However, the buttons at left exist on a flat plane; one button simply looks like a smaller version of the other. There is no information that tells us one is "behind" the other.

At right, however, we can see that the smaller button is located behind the larger one. There's still no way of knowing the distance between them; it could be a slightly smaller globe located a little behind the first one, or a much larger one placed a greater distance away. Add a few shadows and a fake visual horizon, however, and the illusion is produced that the buttons are resting on a receding surface, or floating above it, as you can see in Figure 6-2.

**Figure 6-1.** 3D buttons

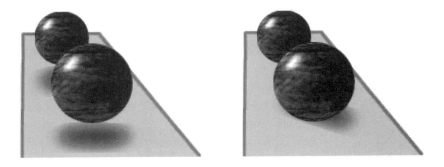

**Figure 6-2.** Adding a horizon and vanishing point

Other visual cues help us discern 3D information. The horizon or vanishing point, as shown in Figure 6-2, exists at some point in a 3D image (whether it's actually shown or just implied), usually "higher" on the picture than the foreground. Objects that are farther away are both smaller and "higher" as they approach the horizon. The shading of the light falling on objects (shadows are shorter the farther away the object is) or even extremely subtle things (e.g., clear air produces a diffusing or "fog" effect that is visible over distant objects) are other clues.

Artists understand all these things, but you and I might not. That's why it's so difficult to create realistic 3D effects from images we create from scratch. The objects we create for our Web pages may not have the visual cues that say "3D" to our brains. We'll learn to add them in the following sections.

# ■ Textures

One key to producing realistic 3D images is using raised textures. You already learned how to use KPT Texture Explorer to create flat, 2D textures (patterns, actually, since we think of textures as having a 3D quality). Here are some easy ways to create true 3D textures; we'll look at methods for using them later on.

### Shiny Metal

You can create a shiny metal look in a few seconds. Just follow these steps:

1. Create a 500 x 500-pixel RGB document at 72 dpi resolution.
2. Choose the Linear Gradient tool (either from the toolbox with Photoshop 5 or by selecting Linear Gradient in Gradient Options with Photoshop 4).
3. From the Gradient drop-down list, select Copper. (This list allows you to choose tones and hues for the gradient, not the *type* of gradient.)
4. Holding down the Shift key, drag from the top of the image to the bottom. A surface with a coppery sheen is produced, as you can see in Figure 6-3.

You might not need copper. You can change the metallic texture to some other metal using these options:

- Use Image | Mode | Grayscale to produce a soft chrome texture. The chrome will look even more realistic if you immediately change the mode back to RGB, then use Image | Adjust | Hue/Saturation. Check the Colorize box, select a blue hue, and reduce saturation so that the chrome has only a hint of a blue cast.
- Image | Adjust | Hue/Saturation can also change your copper to gold or another metal just by moving the Hue slider.

**Figure 6-3.** Coppery metal texture

- Give the metal a brighter shine with Image | Adjust | Brightness/Contrast and increase both values.
- Add some glare with the Render | Lens Flare filter. Choose the 105mm Prime lens setting for the smoothest glare effect. Lens flare produces additional reflections on the surface, which you may want to crop out.
- Apply Kai's Power Tool's Planar Tiling filter using Perspective tiling to achieve a great-looking tubular texture like the one shown in Figure 6-4. You'll have to crop the top half of the image out, as Planar Tiling does its work only in the bottom half of the image.

## Rough Metal

Create a rough metallic effect from the texture you just created by following these steps:

1. Choose Filter | Texture | Texturizer.
2. Select Sandstone from the drop-down Texture list.
3. Move the Scaling slider to 100%.
4. Set the Relief slider to 4. Click OK. You can use the Fade control (Shift+Ctrl/Command-F) to make the texture more subtle if you like. You'll end up with a pitted metal surface like the one shown in Figure 6-5.

**Figure 6-4.** Planar tiling

**Figure 6-5.** Pitted metal surface

## Etched Metal

Creating an etched metal effect can provide a quick introduction to one of Photoshop's more advanced texturizing capabilities. In the preceding project you used the built-in Sandstone texture. Burlap and Canvas textures are also available. However, you can also create your own. Follow these steps to see how.

1. Make a new 500 x 500-pixel grayscale image at 72 dpi resolution.
2. Use Edit|Fill to fill it with a 50% gray tone.
3. Select Filter|Pixelate|Mezzotint, and choose Short Lines from the drop-down list. Click OK to apply the mezzotint effect, shown in Figure 6-6.
4. Press Ctrl/Command+A to select the entire image.
5. Use Layer|Transform|Numeric (Photoshop 4) or Edit|Transform|Numeric (Photoshop 5).
6. In the Rotate area, type in -45 to rotate the image by 45 degrees counter-clockwise. Click OK.
7. Choose a rectangular area from the center of the tilted texture, as shown in Figure 6-7.
8. Save the texture as MetalTex.psd (using Photoshop's native file format).
9. Using a copy of the copper texture you created under Shiny Metal, apply Photoshop's Filter|Texture|Texturizer filter. In the Texture drop-down list, select Load Texture.

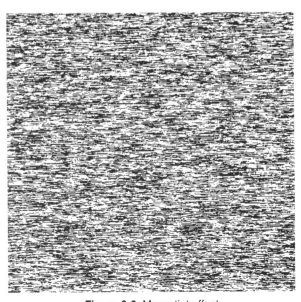

**Figure 6-6.** Mezzotint effect

**Figure 6-7.** Texture turned diagonally

10. Choose MetalTex.psd as the texture to be used for the filter's "bump map."

11. Choose the value you'd like to use for Relief. Figure 6-8 shows the results with Relief values of 4 and 12.

You can use this technique to create textures of your own that can be applied with Photoshop's Texturizer plug-in. Once you've created this metal texture, try one of these variations:

- Photoshop's Texture | Craquelure filter offers melted metal effects like those shown in Figure 6-9.

- Stack light-toned, medium-toned, and dark-toned layers of text one on top of each other, as we did in previous chapters, to create raised or sunken letters like those in Figure 6-10. For a sunken effect, put the dark version on the bottom of the sandwich, offset slightly to the top and left. Place the light version in the middle, offset toward the bottom and right. Put the medium-toned version on top.

# ■ Drop Shadows

Drop shadows are one of the easiest ways of adding a third dimension to a Web graphic. Any image with a shadow behind it seems to pop out of the page and float above its background. We've already used this technique several times in this book. To recap, the best way to make a drop shadow "manually" is to follow these steps:

**Figure 6-8.** Texture applied using different relief values

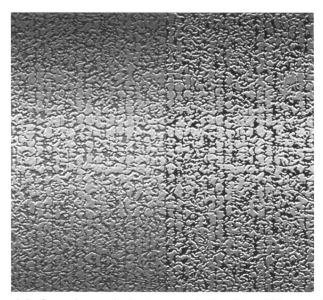

**Figure 6-9.** Craquelure applied using crack depths of 4 and 10, respectively

**Figure 6-10** Etched and raised letters

1. Select the object to be shadowed.
2. Copy the object to the clipboard.
3. Paste the object down in a new layer.
4. Apply a Gaussian blur to that layer, with the Preserve Transparency box unchecked in the Layers palette.
5. Check the Preserve Transparency box and fill the blur with a dark tone, unless you're trying to create a light-colored "glow" around the object. A glow is simply the opposite of a shadow.
6. Paste down a new copy of the object on top of the shadow.
7. Move the shadow, if necessary, so it is cast in the direction you want.

I applied those steps to the image shown in Figure 6-11, with a couple differences. I adjusted the Brightness/Contrast of each nonshadow layer individually, making each brighter and more contrasty than the layer below it. I also used the Sharpen filter on the top two layers, so the bottom, background layer was a little blurry by comparison.

Here are some variations on the traditional shadow technique. In Figure 6-12, you'll find two examples of shadows that fall in front of the object. (In this case, I used text.) In the image at top, the Skew control made the shadow appear as if the light source was directly behind the text. At the bottom, I moved the light source behind and to the side.

**Figure 6-11.** Three dimensions with drop shadows

**Figure 6-12.** Shadows in front of an object, with light source behind (top technique) and behind and to the side (bottom technique)

Even transparent objects can cast shadows.  The image in Figure 6-13 was a complex one and used a whole clutch of different plug-ins to achieve a sci-fi look.  Here's what I did:

- Kai's Power Tools' Planar Tiling filter was applied to the Old-Door.tif file, which you can find in the Chapter 6 folder of the CD-ROM.
- I added clouds to the upper half of the image using Photoshop's Clouds filters, with dark blue and white as the foreground/background colors.
- I created an elliptical selection, filled it with light blue, and then reduced the opacity of the selection's layer to about 50 percent.
- I filled a duplicate of the disk with a darker blue to produce an edge, then moved it slightly below the disk.
- I selected the original disk and used it as a mask to delete everything in the darker disk's layer except for the edge itself.
- Using the marquee tool, I moved the disk selection to a position beneath the disk, blurred it with Gaussian blur, and then filled it with black.
- I adjusted the opacity of the shadow's layer so that the background showed through.

When creating shadows, make sure the shadow conforms to the laws of physics, e.g., it shouldn't fall on the lighter side of the object and

**Figure 6-13.** Transparent objects can cast shadows

should appear to be cast away from the light source. If you use several light sources on an object, you may, in fact, need two shadows. Figure 6-14 shows a realistic shadow. In the color version, included on the CD-ROM packaged with this book, I gave a tint to the shadow that matched the original object, as if the shadow was colored by light bouncing off the object itself.

# ■ Automating Shadows

Even though creating your own shadows isn't difficult, there are quite a few plug-ins that can automate the process for you. Here are a few of them.

## Andromeda Shadow Filter

Andromeda's Shadow filter is by far the most advanced and flexible shadow-making filter on the market. Unlike other products, which create shadows by changing the perspective of a duplicate image (as we did in the previous examples), Andromeda's Shadow Filter uses true 3D geometry that manipulates light sources, the plane the shadow falls on, and the object itself in three-dimensional space before rendering the 2D version you'll use on your Web page.

Just click and drag the shadow in the dialog box shown in Figure 6-15. Edges of the shadow automatically soften and blur the farther a shadow extends from an object, just as they do in real life. This is a dif-

**Figure 6-14.** Try for realism when creating shadows.

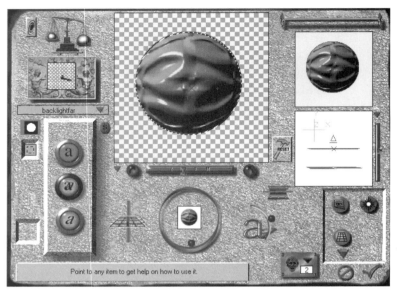

**Figure 6-15.** Andromeda Shadow filter

ficult look to achieve manually, since it's usually easier to apply the same amount of blur to the entire shadow. Andromeda's filter also lets you create multiple light sources (using illumination colors you choose) and change your view of the object using a vertical camera.

Andromeda's shadow filter even comes with a pair of 3D glasses for stereoscopic viewing. The filter has its own unlimited Undo feature, so you can backtrack easily while creating shadow effects even if you haven't upgraded to Photoshop 5.

## Eye Candy Drop Shadow

Eye Candy's Drop Shadow filter is best used for creating shadows that fall underneath the object, rather than those that extend far in front of it. Our results weren't very realistic when creating anything other than simple drop shadows. However, this filter works very fast and allows you to adjust shadow angle, size, opacity, amount of blur, and shadow color. There are 14 presets that cover most drop shadow varieties, so if you have a button you need to shadow quickly, this may be your best bet. Figure 6-16 shows the Eye Candy Drop Shadow dialog box.

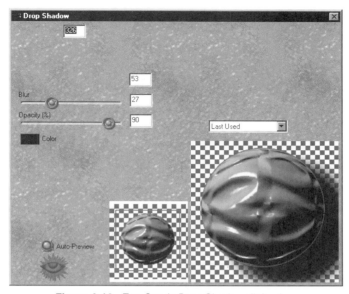

**Figure 6-16.** Eye Candy Drop Shadow dialog box

## Extensis PhotoCastShadow

Extensis's PhotoCastShadow filter has a few more controls than Eye Candy's and, most importantly, lets you differentiate between drop shadows (those that seem to appear below a floating object) and cast shadows (those that appear to have been cast behind the object from a light source in front). This plug-in includes all the settings found in the Eye Candy Drop Shadow filter, with many extras. You can, for example, use an eye dropper tool to extract a color for the shadow from a large preview window.

Extensis' tool allows both conventional blur and perspective blur—the kind that can be adjusted using skew controls and gets softer the farther a shadow extends from an object. Rotation angle, direction, length, and X/Y offsets can be typed in manually, giving you a great deal of control and repeatability. When PhotoCastShadow is set for real-time rendering, it can take awhile for the preview to appear, but the results are worth the wait. Figure 6-17 shows an example of what this filter can do.

## Ulead Drop Shadow

Available free with PhotoImpact or separately as part of the Ulead Web.Plugins package, Ulead's Drop Shadow filter is a bare-bones drop shadow tool that may be the fastest to use because of its simplicity.

**Figure 6-17.** Extensis PhotoCastShadow filter

You can check a radio button to specify placement of the shadow, type in x and y offset, set opacity, and enter the amount of edge blending you want (in pixels). If all you need are quick drop shadows, this product (shown in Figure 6-18) or Eye Candy may be all you need.

# ■ Instant Bevels

In previous chapters, I've showed you how to create beveled edges for buttons, text, and other objects. There's a quicker way that can produce interesting 3D surfaces in a few seconds. You can apply the effect to freehand drawings and text (as you can see in Figure 6-19) or to objects of any shape (as in Figure 6-20). In all cases, you'll follow these steps:

1. Create the text or drawing you want to add a bevel to onto a transparent layer, using white as your foreground color. The image may be a little difficult to see now, but it's important to use white.
2. Use Select|Load Selection and choose the layer's transparency from the Channel drop-down list.
3. Use Select|Feather, and feather the selection. I used a value of six pixels for my example.
4. Save the new selection under a name you'll remember.
5. Now choose Filter|Render|Lighting Effects. In the Texture Channel drop-down list, select the name of the selection you just saved. Set the height slider to Mountainous.

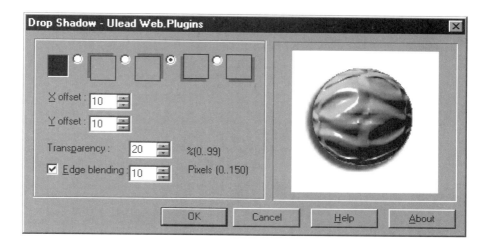

**Figure 6-18.** Ulead's Drop Shadow filter

**Figure 6-19.** Lighting Effect applied to freehand drawing and text

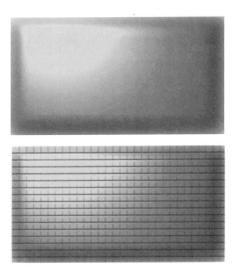

**Figure 6.20** Lighting Effect applied to plain white rectangle (top) and to rectangle given texture with Patchwork plug-in.

**Figure 6-21.** Other bevel effects

6. Apply a lighting effect of your choice. Be sure and apply a color to the light source if you want your object to be something other than white. Click OK, and you're done.

Don't forget about the bevels and 3D effects you can create with Eye Candy, Extensis PhotoTools, or Ulead's Buttonizer. We covered these effects in Chapter 5. More examples of what you can do are shown in Figure 6-21.

# ■ Moving On

This chapter served as an introduction to 3D effects you can achieve with plug-ins. But we're far from through with three-dimensional techniques. Because 3D is applied to type so often, I'm going to devote an entire chapter to cool type effects, particularly those that give your fonts texture and relief. I'll even show you an easy way to produce 3D text that really jumps off the page—if your visitors remember to use their red/blue 3D glasses!

# 7

# Rules and Other Web Artifacts

Rules are one of the most effective design elements you can add to a Web page. The built-in rules allowed by HTML often look good and are quick to download (since they are nothing more than HTML instructions for your browser), but only a few variations in width and style are possible.

Graphics rules offer more possibilities. Although these rules must be downloaded before they can be displayed, because they're lean and lithe, rules can be sprinkled about a Web page to separate elements without wasting a great deal of your visitors' time. These elements can be stored in a visitor's browser's cache, so when they're reused on the same or different pages, the browser can display them almost instantly.

Moreover, a consistent use of rules can unify your page by creating a visual theme, whether it's warm and homey or modern and high-tech. You can develop rules built on the same graphic foundation, but with slight variations that can characterize different kinds of content.

Rules aren't the only low-overhead graphic elements you can add to a page. Navigation icons—a kind of button—as well as frames and special edges added to images also provide visual interest with almost no extra time required to download them. In this chapter, we're going to explore nearly two dozen different effects you can use to create interesting Web page objects using plug-ins.

# ■ In This Chapter

- Rules for Rules
- Creative Rules
- Navigation Icons
- Other Shapes
- Image Maps
- Creating the Map Graphic
- Frames
- Graphic Edges

# ■ Rules for Rules

Rules, navigation icons, frames, and edges all offer their own creative potential. You'll probably use rules most. They are simply horizontal graphics a few pixels tall, and either wide enough to be centered in the middle of a browser window or so wide that the rule extends from edge to edge. Here are some quick tips for using rules on your Web pages:

- If you want to be sure a rule will be centered in your Web page window, make it smaller than 600 pixels wide to improve the chances that it will be narrower than the window even if your visitor is using 640 x 480 resolution. That's no guarantee, of course, as visitors can reduce their browser window to any size they like. You might have a 400-pixel-wide window displayed on a 1024 x 768 screen, for example, although that might not be likely. Remember to use the HTML CENTER tag to position the rule evenly.

- If you'd like the rule to extend the full width of the browser window, make it wider than you'll need—for example, 1200 pixels wide. The browser will trim the excess.

- Rules can be created as transparent GIFs or JPEG files. If you use a transparent GIF as a rule, the rule can have holes or gaps in it. You could, for example, create a dotted line rule that allowed the background image to show through, as you can see in Figure 7-1. We'll use this technique to create a bubbly rule later in this chapter.

- Use JPEGs as rules when you want to include a full range of tones beyond the 216/256 that can be incorporated into a GIF.

- Rules must have hard edges, except when you use "fake" transparency to help them blend into the background. In this case, the background color must be the same as the surrounding color of the rule, so the two will blend, as you can see in Figure 7-2.

**Figure 7-1.** Transparent GIF as rule

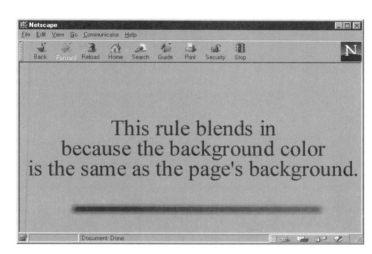

**Figure 7-2.**   Because the rule's background is the same color as the page's background, it blends in seamlessly even though it has fuzzy edges.

# ■ Creative Rules

The best part about making your own rules, is that you can defy your regulations any time you like and the concept applies just as well to the Web.  Here are some easy techniques you can use to create your own custom rules.

## Abstract Art

For the example shown in Figure 7-3, I wanted a modernistic, abstract rule. You can create one of your own by following these steps:

1.  First create a rectangle that is both narrower and taller than the rule you want to end up with.

2.  Fill the shape with a light color, then daub on some random brush strokes. The exact pattern doesn't matter, but if you're more artistic than I am, you can indulge yourself.

3.  Next, apply a pixelation filter of your choice to give the pattern an appearance recalling a bad abstract painter (the kind who becomes *less* well-known after death).

4.  Using Photoshop's Scale command (found under Layer | Transform with Photoshop 4, and Edit | Transform with Photoshop 5), squeeze the rectangle down to the height you want for your rule—generally about 10 pixels high. Stretch it out to the width required.

5.  Give the rule a tubular appearance by brushing the top and bottom edges with the Burn tool, and lightening the center of the rule with the Dodge tool.

**Figure 7-3.** Abstract rule

**Color 17.** To change etched into raised letters, just reverse the angle of the apparent light source.

**Color 18.** Shadows in front of an object, with light source behind (top) and behind and to the side (bottom). Both are described in Chapter 6.

**Color 19.** Even transparent objects can cast shadows!

**Color 20.** Bevel effects

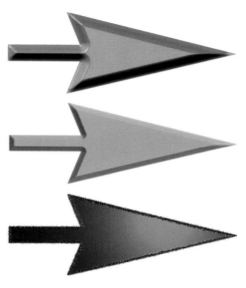

**Color 21.** Chapter 7 shows how to create sharp-looking arrows using Photoshop's Line tool and several plug-ins.

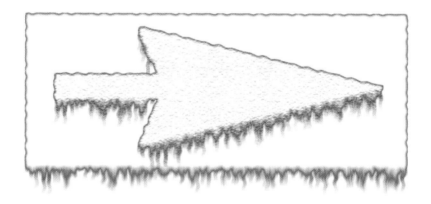

**Color 22.** Ulead's Snow plug-in created this frigid look.

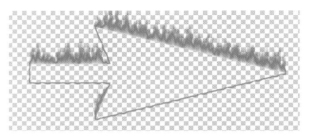
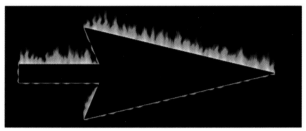

**Color 23.** Ulead's Fire filter created this flaming arrow.

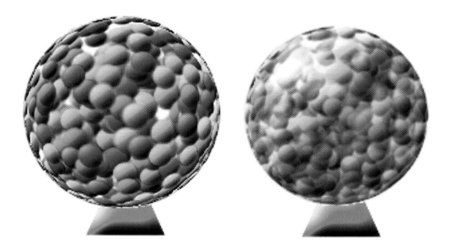

**Color 24.** A collection of colored spheres and KPT's Glass Lens filter are all you need to create a gumball machine.

**Color 25.** Photoshop's Wind filter applied to featured edge four different times

**Color 26.** Flaming text with Ulead's Fire filter

**Color 27.** Irregular selections and Eye Candy's Inner Bevel filter are all you need to produce a corroded effect.

**Color 28.** Two versions of snowy text, using a variety of plug-ins described in Chapter 8

**Color 29.** Several gradients and a Lens Flare filter create a nameplate.

**Color 30.** Photoshop's own Lighting Effects filter creates dramatic lighting and texture effects.

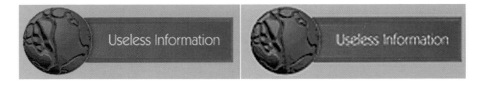

**Color 31.** The original image (left) has been reduced and then enlarged to original size to show how much information is lost to interpolation.

**Color 32.** Original photos (left) processed with Spatter filter (right)

## Alternate Method

I like using Burn and Dodge to produce tubular effects because the slight variations in tone caused by irregular hand movements have an organic appearance.  If you don't mind perfection, here's a quick way to produce the tube effect without bothering with the Burn and Dodge tools:

1. Start with a rectangular selection, as shown at the top of Figure 7-4. Fill it with a dark tone.
2. Use Select | Modify | Contract to reduce the size of the selection. I used a value of 6 to contract my selection.
3. Use Select | Feather to blend the smaller selection smoothly.  I used a value of 6 in this case.
4. Fill the feathered selection with a lighter tone.  You'll end up with the shading effect shown at the bottom of Figure 7-4.  You can apply the plug-in of your choice to finish the rule.

## Shiny Tube

For a variation on this effect, fill the rectangle with a gradient, and apply the lightening/darkening *before* you squeeze the rule down to its finished size, as you can see at the bottom of Figure 7-5.  This technique compresses the gradation so the rule has a shiny appearance, as shown at the top of the figure.  Simply lightening and darkening as we did earlier produces the softer effect shown in the middle.

**Figure 7-4.** Fast shading technique

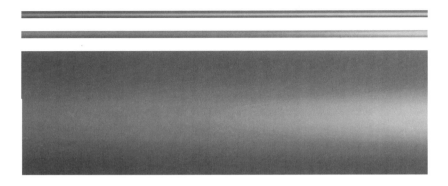

**Figure 7-5.** Bottom: Gradient lightened and darkened before rectangle is squeezed. Center: Conventional lightening and darkening. Top: The shiny tube effect achieved by squeezing the rectangle at bottom.

## Textured Rules

Try applying textures to your rules. The texture should complement the texture of the background. For example, you won't want to place a homey thatched rule on top of a high-tech, shiny background. Two examples are shown in Figure 7-6. For the top version, I filled the rule with a light blue tone, and then applied Photoshop's Graphic Pen plug-in. For the bottom example, I used Eye Candy's Weave filter.

## Transparent GIF Rules

One underused effect is to create rules from transparent GIFs. The technique gives you a great deal of flexibility, since the rule can appear to float above your background rather than be embedded in it. Keep in mind that transparent GIFs must have a hard edge, as only one color can be transparent. That means that soft, anti-aliased edges will show up and spoil the transparent effect. While the PNG format allows transparent images that smoothly blend with the background, it isn't widely supported by the most common browsers.

To create a transparent GIF rule, follow these steps:

1. Create the rule—including one color and one color only—that you want to drop out. Figure 7-7 shows two examples. For the top example, I created a plain blue rule and filled it with bubbles using a Ulead Web.plugins Particle effect. I copied the rule to a new, empty layer; then I selected the blue surrounding area and de-

**Figure 7-6.** Textured rules using Photoshop's Graphic Pen and Eye Candy Weave filters

**Figure 7-7.** Two transparent GIF rules

leted it, leaving the bubbles on a transparent background.  For the bottom effect, I filled the rule with a plain blue, then applied Kai's Power Tools' Glass Lens effect, and deleted the surrounding area once more.

2. With the layer containing the transparent rule active, select File | Export | GIF89a Export and save the file as a transparent GIF.

## More Shaded Rules

Any of the tools we used in previous chapters to create 3D buttons and objects can be applied to rules as well.  Extensis PhotoTools' PhotoEmboss filter, shown in Figure 7-8, is an excellent tool for building 3D rules quickly. For the rule at the top of Figure 7-9, I selected a thin strip from a photograph, almost at random, and then applied the PhotoEmboss filter to it.  For the bottom example, I applied the plug-in to a plain yellow rectangle. In both cases, I used the filter's Cutout mode.

To achieve the effects in Figure 7-10, just use your favorite automatic button filter, like those included in Ulead's Web.plugins package, Extensis PhotoTools, or one of Eye Candy's multiple buttonizer options.

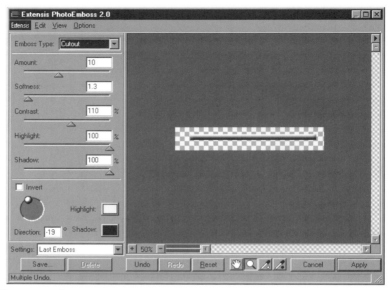

**Figure 7-8.** Select Cutout in Extensis PhotoTools' PhotoEmboss filter's dialog box

**Figure 7-9.** Two shaded rules produced with PhotoEmboss

**Figure 7-10.** Bevels make great rules.

# ■ Navigation Icons

Arrows can point your visitors to the hot spots on your site, or move them from page to page. If you've tried to make an interesting arrow icon from scratch, you know how tedious the job can be. However, Photoshop has all the tools built in to create the arrow itself, and your plug-ins can add the interest you require to lure visitors into clicking on the navigation button. Here are some effects you can achieve in no time at all.

## Basic Arrow

Unless you've needed some callouts for your images, you may have never used Photoshop's arrowheads feature of the Line tool. The effect can be activated within the Line Options dialog box. You may select the thickness of the line (the arrowhead will be sized proportionately, automatically), whether you want the arrowhead anti-aliased (your best choice if you are not creating a transparent GIF), and whether you want the arrowhead placed at the start or end (or both) of the line you drag.

You may also edit the shape of the arrowhead by clicking the Shape button in the dialog box, as you can see in Figure 7-11. Parameters you may enter include width (how thick the arrowhead is in relation to the line), the length (how far along the line it extends), and the amount of concavity (the angle of the back of the arrow from the shaft). The cool

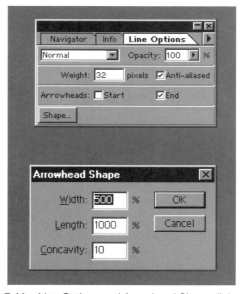

**Figure 7-11.** Line Options and Arrowhead Shape dialog boxes

part about the arrow tool is that just by dragging in different ways, you can create a navigation arrow at any angle or even create an arrow point without the shaft, as shown in Figure 7-12. To create a vertical or horizontal arrow, just hold down the shift key while you drag.

As you might expect, the same plug-ins that can be used to create rules and buttons can be applied to navigation arrows as well. Here are some variations you'll want to try. In Figure 7-13, a plain-vanilla arrow is shown at the top. In the middle is the same arrow, with Eye Candy's Carve filter applied, producing an interesting concave effect. I set the Bevel Width to 20 pixels, and selected Rounded bevel shape. Smoothness was set to 5, Shadow Depth to 19, and the Darken Depths control to 32. Next, I applied Eye Candy's Fur filter to the carved arrow, generating yet another interesting look.

For Figure 7-14, I tried out three more filters. At the top, I applied Eye Candy's Inner Bevel, using a Bevel Width of 20 pixels, and Rounded bevel shape, with smoothness set to 5, and Shadow Depth to 50. You can set the lighting direction and brightness of the highlight to your taste with this filter. The middle variation was created using Ulead Web.plugins' Buttonizer (Any Shape) plug-in. At the bottom is an arrow rendered using nothing more than Web.plugins' Concrete texture.

**Figure 7-12.** Arrowhead variations

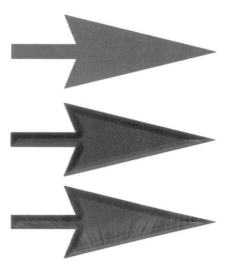

**Figure 7-13.** Plain arrow (top), Inner Bevel (middle), and Inner Bevel with Fur filter applied (bottom)

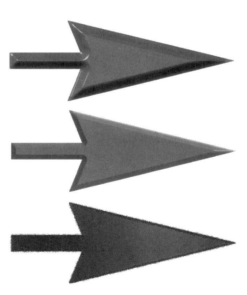

**Figure 7-14.** More arrows

## Hot and Cold Running Arrows

Although I'll show you how to create fire and ice effects using only Photoshop's build-in filters later on, if you have Ulead's Web.plugins package, the Type Effects filter can apply these eye-catching effects with a few clicks. If you want to create navigation arrows that point visitors toward your site's personal hot spots or very cool pages, you can create one of these icons yourself by following these instructions. Start with the frozen arrow first.

1. Create a basic arrow using the Line tool, as previously described.
2. Fill the arrow with white, and make a copy on the clipboard.
3. Apply The Type Effects Snow filter. Icicles dripping from the lower edges will magically appear.
4. Paste down the copy you made.
5. Select the copy's layer, and with Preserve Transparency checked, apply the Texture | Texturizer filter, using the Sandstone texture. Given the right hue, sandstone looks a lot like frozen snow.
6. Merge the layers so the icy arrow and sandstone texture are combined.
7. Create a rectangular selection outside the arrow.
8. Apply the Type Effects Snow filter to the surrounding rectangle.
9. Flatten the image.
10. If the image has a color cast, remove it by selecting Image | Adjust | Desaturate (or press Shift+Command/Ctrl+U).
11. Use Adjust | Image | Hue/Saturation to apply a light blue cast to the image. Your image should look like the variation at top in Figure 7-15.

The flaming arrow is a little trickier, but doesn't take very long to finish.

1. Create the arrow as you just did, onto a transparent layer.
2. Apply the Type Effects Fire filter. Remember that to use this filter you must not have the Preserve Transparency button checked. The filter needs to use any transparent area in your image to apply the flames. The intermediate flaming arrow will look like the example at the top of Figure 7-16.
3. Fill the center of the arrow with black.
4. Create a new layer underneath the flaming arrow, and fill it with black.
5. Flatten the image to produce the burning arrow you see at the bottom of Figure 7-16.

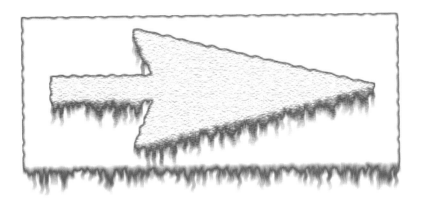

**Figure 7-15.** Frozen arrow

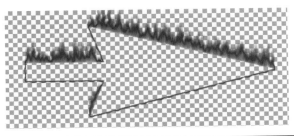

**Figure 7-16.** Flaming arrow

# ■ Other Shapes

Objects created for your Web page can be any shape you like, particularly if you save them as transparent GIFs that float on your page's background image. Plug-ins can help produce professional-looking effects like the ones in this section.

## Water Drops

Photoshop's Emboss filter, applied to a group of irregular rounded shapes, can produce a fair simulation of water droplets, particularly if you use the Hue/Saturation controls to add a blue tint. However, if you have Extensis PhotoTools, you can get even better effects. Just follow these steps:

1. Use the lasso tool to create splashes on a transparent layer as a series of selections. Hold down the Shift key to select several areas. Don't be too concerned about producing smooth, rounded corners.
2. Apply Photoshop's Select | Modify | Smooth option to the selection. Choose a value of 16 pixels (the maximum available) to create smoothly rounded drops.
3. Fill the selected areas with a tone that represents the liquid inside the drops (e.g., blue for water, green for Flubber) Your image should look something like Figure 7-17.

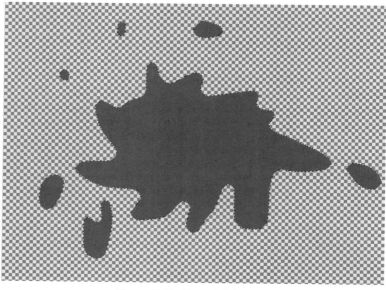

**Figure 7-17.** Rounded droplets

4. Apply Extensis PhotoTools' PhotoEmboss filter. Choose Cutout for the emboss type, 10 for the Amount, 4 for Softness, and 110 percent for Contrast, and leave Highlight and Shadow at 100 percent each.

You can save the image as a transparent GIF that will allow the background to show through around each drop, or you can do as I did for Figure 7-18, and layer the liquid on top of a rough background. I changed the opacity of the drops to about 50 percent to allow the background to show through.

## Gumballs

A variation on this effect can produce gumballs instead of a liquid. For the next example, I dotted a transparent layer with multiple discs, using the paintbrush and a hard-edged brush tip, as you can see at left in Figure 7-19. Then I applied the PhotoEmboss filter to create rounded spheres. I selected groups of the gumballs and colored them with bright hues, as you could see at right in Figure 7-19 by looking at the full-color version of the illustration. Finally, I copied the gumballs multiple times, offsetting them slightly each time to create the cluster you can see at the bottom of Figure 7-19.

If you want a gumball machine effect, make a circular selection, delete everything outside the selection, and then apply either Photoshop's

**Figure 7-18.** Drops on a background

**Figure 7-19.** Creating gumballs

Spherize filter to get the effect shown at left in Figure 7-20, or Kai's Power Tools' Glass Lens filter (set to Soft) to produce the shiny globe shown at right in Figure 7-20.

# ■ Image Maps

Image maps—graphics with embedded "hot spots" visitors click to activate a hyperlink—can be the foundation of sleek, sinewy, and highly intuitive Web pages. Why rely on boring old buttons or text links, when you can incorporate multiple gateways to your site in an eye-catching graphic?

An image map is a graphic that has been divided into areas or regions a browser or Web server can recognize, using visible or invisible "borders" you define using a simple X/Y coordinate system. An image map could use an actual map as a graphic—say, an outline of the United States, with each state or region corresponding to a hyperlink to your company's sales information for that state. Or, the boundaries within the image map can be more amorphous. A medical Web page might have an anatomical chart that links to other pages whenever a visitor clicks in the neighborhood of a particular structure.

As with chocolate and fast sports cars, there's a downside to all the excitement. Clickable image maps are perhaps the most under-used, least well understood, and most often badly applied graphic elements

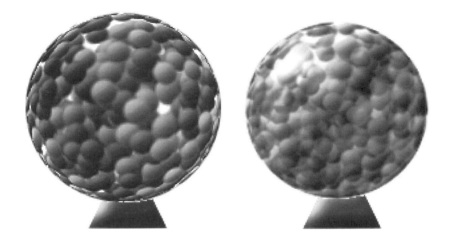

**Figure 7-20.** Spherize and Glass Lens filters producing gumball machine globes.

you're likely to find on a Web page.   Even so, you can put these graphics to work for you effectively if you follow a few guidelines.

Reasonably sized image maps—under 50K or so—can make your site easier to navigate. A humongous graphic, whether used as a map or not, can convert a page into a nightmare that invites a Back button bailout even before the image completes its creep down a visitor's screen. Another factor limiting the use of image maps is that they come in two flavors: server-side, in which all the work is done by a CGI script on the host computer, and the potentially faster, easier-to-implement client-side map, which is activated by each visitor's browser.

What makes a good image map? First of all, you want an alluring graphic that attracts visitors' attention. It should convey some information about the links nestled inside the image and, most importantly, look enough like an image map to invite clicking. Visitors find nothing more frustrating than clickworthy images that contain no links, or hidden image maps that are stumbled upon by accident.  An actual map, a dashboard full of buttons, a control panel, or similar graphics all make good image maps.  Abstract shapes, unlabeled images, and large files that take a long time to download are poor choices for this technique. And don't forget to include text links for nonimage-capable browsers. If all your links are embedded in image maps, even a Netscape Navigator user who has shut off image display will be lost on your page.

No mystic HTML incantations are needed to invoke this magic. The secret is in a simple ASCII file that contains little more than the coordinates of points defining any regions you want, and the URL or link to be activated when a visitor clicks inside that area. You'll find descriptions of how to put together these files in any good HTML guide. However, actually collecting the list of coordinates can be tricky—although there are several Photoshop plug-ins that can help you streamline this task.

# ■ Creating the Map Graphic

First, create the graphic you want to use as an image map. You could use a boring old line map like the one at left in Figure 7-21, an outline of Ohio, the home state of a well-known computer book author. You can find the file on the CD-ROM packaged with this book as Ohio.tif.

I spiced up the image by applying Eye Candy's Chrome filter, with Softness set at 24, Variation at 19, Contrast at 100, and number of bands at 2. You would also give the map a 3D look by applying Photoshop's Emboss filter, followed by a bevel-making plug-in of your choice, as shown in Figure 7-22.

If you have Ulead's Web.Plugins, you can use it to generate the HTML code to define a portion of the map for the image map file. Use the Lasso tool to select the area you want set aside as a clickable por-

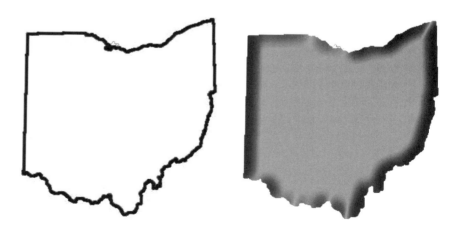

**Figure 7-21.** Eye Candy's Chrome filter applied to a map

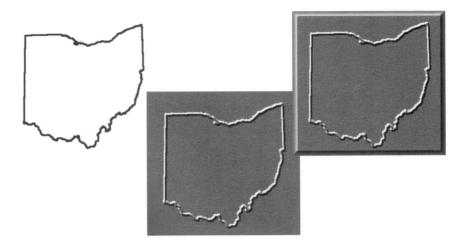

**Figure 7-22.** Emboss filter produces a 3D look.

tion of the map. Then choose the Image Map Tag plug-in, and copy the information to the clipboard, using the button included in the plug-in's dialog box, as in Figure 7-23.

Paste the HTML code down in your favorite HTML editor. Then rinse, lather, and repeat to define additional clickable areas.

# ■ Frames

Frames—the graphic kind, not the HTML variety—can call attention to specific images on your page. It's probably not a good idea to use more than one graphic frame on a page, but put to work judiciously, they can add an interesting design element. Extensis has an excellent frame-making plug-in with PhotoFrame, while Ulead includes a frame filter with PhotoImpact and in its add-on Web.Plugins filter package. Here are some examples of frames you can create using plug-ins.

The easiest frame is just a button with the center cut out and replaced by another graphic. Figure 7-24 shows that kind of frame, created using Extensis PhotoTools' PhotoBevel plug-in.

Ulead's Web.Plug-ins set includes a Frame and Shadow filter that generates a frame from your selection, and includes a library of textures, similar to those in Kai's Power Tools' Texture Explorer, that you can apply. Figure 7-25 shows the filter's dialog box.

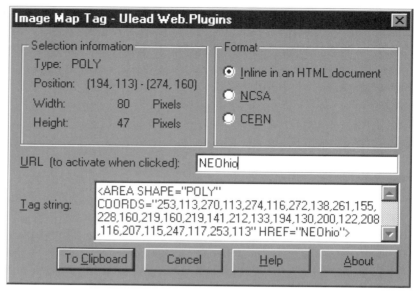

**Figure 7-23.** Ulead's Image Map Tag plug-in

**Figure 7-24.** Beveled button as a frame

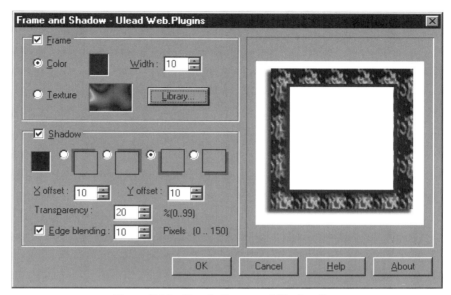

**Figure 7-25.** Ulead's Frame and Shadow filter

Real picture frames often have a double matte—an inner matte of a particular color or pattern, plus a larger matte of a different color or matte. Figure 7-26 shows an example of this kind of frame, also produced using Ulead's Frame and Shadow filter.

I put together a more conventional double matte using Eye Candy's Inner Bevel filter on the inner mask, and then applying Photoshop's Texturizer filter with a Canvas texture to the surrounding matte. You can see the results in Figure 7-27.

# ■ Graphic Edges

While you can purchase plug-ins that do nothing but create cool edge effects for your graphics, some great looks can be achieved using your current filter sets. The next few examples show what you can do. All were based on the photo at left in Figure 7-28. I selected the edge of the image, and applied the Select|Feather option with a value of 32. Then, at right in the same figure, is the photo with Photoshop's Diffuse Glow filter applied.

I've created two different kinds of edges to the photo in Figure 7-29. At left is a version with Photoshop's Glass filter applied, using a distortion value of 13. At right, I applied the Photoshop Spatter filter.

**Figure 7-26.** Double-matte frame

**Figure 7-27.** Conventional photographic double matte

**Figure 7-28.** Unmodified image (left) and image with Diffuse Glow applied to feathered edge (right)

**Figure 7-29.** Edges created with Photoshop's Glass and Spatter filters applied to feathered edge

Eye Candy's Swirl filter is an intriguing plug-in that you'll want to play with.  I used it to create a dreamy frame for the test photo.  My results are shown in Figure 7-30.

The final edge effect seen in Figure 7-31 might puzzle you until you find out how I rendered it.  Believe it or not, I applied Photoshop's Wind filter (although Kai's Power Tool's PixelWeather filter would also work).  The trick here is to apply the filter four different times, rotating the im-

**Figure 7-30.**  Edge created with Eye Candy's Swirl filter

**Figure 7-31.**  Photoshop's Wind filter applied to feathered edge four different times

age 90 degrees each time. You'll end up with an image like the one in Figure 7-31. After you've used the Wind-type filters for a while, you'll see just how versatile they are. As you'll see in Chapter 11, I also like to use this plug-in to create painterly strokes on images.

# ◼ Moving On

In the next chapter, we'll combine much of what we've learned in previous sections to create interesting type effects with texture, 3D realism, and other eye-catching features. You'll learn how to create text that jumps out from the page using plug-ins and Photoshop 5's new type features.

chapter

# 8

# Using Filters with Text

In this chapter I'll show you some ways filters can be used to liven up the graphic text you place on your Web pages. It's easy to create 3D text, add metallic textures, and perform other magic if you just know how.

As you realize, Web browsers are limited in the ways they can display fonts. Your Web page can size type using H1, H2, H3 (and so forth) headings that theoretically should control the size of the font, but in reality visitors are free to tell their browsers to use a smaller type size than you might expect for any or all headings. The actual fonts displayed are usually limited to plain vanilla serif and sans-serif styles, although the new cascading style sheet specification in HTML 4.0 does allow specifying just about any font—but that typeface will be used only if it also exists on the visitor's computer.

Still, you can put any font you like on your Web page as long as you're willing to convert it to graphics. This chapter will show you how to add life to your fonts with special effects that plug-ins can provide.

## ■ In This Chapter

- Working with Text
- Elemental Techniques
- New Type Tools

## ■ Working with Text

The TrueType and Adobe Type 1 fonts installed on your computer lead a dual life. For word processing and most other applications, they exist as scalable fonts; that is, you can take any particular font outline and enlarge or reduce it to virtually any type size that will fit on your screen. That means you can add type to images as small as a few points or as large as several hundred points, depending on the resolution of your image.

However, with Photoshop prior to Version 5.0 and most other image editors, once you've created some text and pasted it down into your image, it becomes a part of that image (even if pasted into a layer) and is converted into a bitmap that can't be resized without adding or removing the pixels used to draw the letter. Ordinarily, enlarging or reducing anything potentially produces jaggies, but with text the resizing will be particularly noticeable, since the diagonal strokes found in many characters are the first to succumb to stair-stepping.

You'll find that graphical text usually looks best with some kind of anti-aliasing applied. Figure 8-1 shows an example of text as it appears with and without this smoothing. Most of the projects in this chapter will use anti-aliasing, blending, and a full range of colors to make the text look its best. You'll find that something as simple as a texture can hide imperfections in your online text.

**Figure 8-1.** Unaliased (left) and aliased (right) text

# ■ Elemental Techniques

Here are several techniques you can use to recreate the forces of nature, in terms of lightning, fire, and snow. Even if you have fire or snow filters available as add-ons, you'll find these methods are even more flexible. Although we're applying them to text, you can use any of these to dress up buttons, backgrounds, edges, or other Web artifacts.

## Lightning Reflexes

To create bolts of lighting within your text, just follow these steps:

1. Open a 600 x 600-pixel RGB image with 72-dpi resolution.
2. Use Edit | Fill and select 50% Gray from the Use: pull-down list in the Contents area of the dialog box, and then apply to the image.
3. Apply the Clouds filter to your image, and then process it again immediately with Difference Clouds.
4. Use Image | Adjust | Invert to reverse the image, so all the dark edges formed by the clouds now become streaks of white.
5. Use Image | Adjust | Auto Levels to accentuate the streaks, making them resemble lightning, as shown in Figure 8-2.
6. Use the Hue/Saturation control with the Colorize box checked to add color to your lightning bolts. Deep yellows, magentas, and blues all work well. I selected a dark blue by moving the Hue slider and then bumped up Saturation to 78 percent. You can also ad-

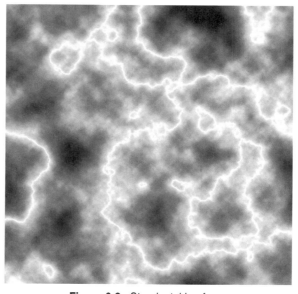

**Figure 8-2.** Streaks taking form

just the Lightness slider to get different effects depending on
whether you've set Lightness high or low. I moved it to +25 to
add some background, as you can see in Figure 8-3.

7. Add some text using Photoshop's Type Mask tool. I used a 92-point
serif font.

8. With the Marquee tool selected, move the type mask around until it over-
laps an area of the background with vivid lightning bolts.

9. Copy a type-shaped section of the background using the type mask tool,
and then paste down into a new layer.

10. Select Edit | Transform | Numeric (with Photoshop 5) or Layer | Trans-
form | Numeric (with Photoshop 4) and enter 125% into the
Width box in the Scale area. Check the Constrain box, and click
OK. Your lightning-filled type will grow.

11. Add a glow behind the text using one of the following methods:
    - Use Eye Candy's Glow filter, set to a width of 11, Opacity of
      75%, Drop off of Fat, and a contrasting color of your choice.
    - Apply Extensis's PhotoGlow filter, set to a Glow Type of
      Edge; Stroke Shape: Round; Stroke Width: 7; Radiance: 4;
      Opacity 75%; and a contrasting glow color of your choice.

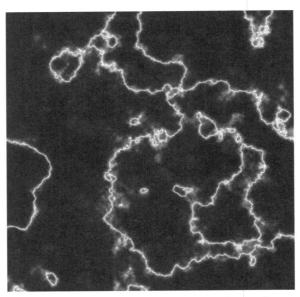

**Figure 8-3.** Colorized lightning and background

- If you have neither of these filters, use the drop shadow method described in the beginning of Chapter 7: Copy the text again, add Gaussian blur, fill with a light contrasting color, and move behind the original text to provide a glow.

The results are shown in Figure 8-4. Underneath is another version, created by adding a nonblurred drop "shadow" in white before the blurry shadow was added. I then lightened the text and darkened the background using Levels before I flattened the image.

## Hot Spots

If you have Ulead's Web.Plugins, you can create a variety of great fire effects. To create a fire effect for your type, follow these easy steps:

1. Create a new, blank image measuring 600 x 600 pixels with 72-dpi resolution in RGB mode.
2. Use the Type Mask tool to enter your text as a selection. I used the words "Hot Spots" to indicate links to hot spots on the Web.
3. Fill the text with black and copy it to the clipboard.
4. Apply Ulead's Text Effects filter, choosing the Fire option. You'll have an effect like the one shown in Figure 8-5.
5. Paste down the copy of the text you made in Step 3.
6. Use Transform | Numeric (found in either the Edit or Layer menu, depending on whether you have Photoshop 5 or 4) and scale the type to 75 of the original size.

**Figure 8-4.** Charged text

**Figure 8-5.** Initial flame effect

7. Apply the Text Effects fire filter once more, and move the flaming smaller text up and behind the original text.
8. Paste down the text once again, and repeat Steps 6 and 7, but scaling the text to 50 percent of the original size.
9. Using the Brush, draw a wavy line underneath all the text.
10. Apply the Text Effects fire filter to it, as well.
11. Create a new layer underneath all the flaming layers, and fill it with black.
12. Flatten the image. It should look something like Figure 8-6.

## Great White North

Some spots aren't so hot—but they still can be cool. You can create frozen text that positively drips with coolness if you know which plug-ins to use. Follow these steps to duplicate my own favorite wintery text.

1. Create a new, blank image measuring 600 x 600 pixels with 72 dpi resolution in RGB mode.
2. Use the Type Mask tool to enter your text as a selection. I used the words "Maximum Cool " to indicate links to very cool spots on my Web site.
3. Fill the text with any color (it doesn't matter) and copy it to the clipboard.

**Figure 8-6.** Finished flaming text

4. Apply the Ulead Type Effects filter, using the Snow option and a Strength setting of 4.
5. Create a new empty layer and place it underneath the text layer on the Layers palette.
6. Choose blue as a foreground color, leaving white as the background color.
7. With the Linear Gradient tool, drag from the bottom to the top of the image.
8. Apply Photoshop's Texture | Texturizer to the background gradient, using the Sandstone texture set to a Relief value of 1.
9. Make sure the text layer is selected, and then rotate it using Transform | Rotate 90 degrees CW (clockwise).
10. Apply Photoshop's Wind filter, set to Stagger and From the Left.
11. Use Transform | Rotate 90 degrees CCW to return the text to its original orientation.
12. Apply the shadow filter of your choice. I used Andromeda Shadow, shown in Figure 8-7.
13. Crop your image to arrive at an effect like the one shown in Figure 8-8.

## Decay

If you want a rough, corroded metallic look, all you need is your favorite buttonizer plug-in and some text to destroy. Follow these steps to produce a unique decayed look.

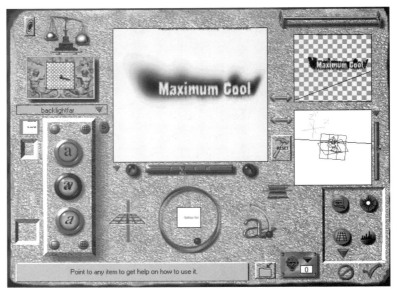

**Figure 8-7.** Andromeda Shadow filter

**Figure 8-8.** Frozen text

1. On a new, transparent RGB document, create your text with the **Text Mask** tool and fill it with a medium hue, such as blue.
2. With the text still selected, use the Lasso while holding down the **Alt/Op-** tion key to deselect parts of the text. Try to produce areas that look like cracks or pitted areas, as you can see in Figure 8-9.

3. Apply the buttonizer.  I used Eye Candy's Inner Bevel and set the depth and contrast settings high to produce a deeply chiseled effect.
4. Invert the selection and apply Photoshop's Texture|Texturizer Sandstone filter.  You'll wind up with the great-looking effect shown in Figure 8-10.

## Creating a Metal Look

You'll often want to create text with a metallic sheen, especially when you want a futuristic or industrial look.  Metal also enhances illustrations with mechanical things or robots, and can be used to simulate sil-

**Figure 8-9.**  Selected pits and cracks

**Figure 8-10.**  Finished corroded text

ver or gold. This first effect, shown in Figure 8-11, produces an icy-blue metal surface. You can easily reproduce this look with Photoshop's Chrome filter. Although this illustration is in black and white, you can check out the original image on the CD-ROM to get the full effect. To produce this text, follow these steps:

1. Place the word *Metal* in a new image, using a thick font like the Copperplate I used. This is a very common all-caps font with an engraved look that is favored for advertising because of its elegance.
2. Save the selection, so you can work with the text separately from the background.
3. Fill the text with a medium gray. (Use Edit | Fill and choose 50 percent gray in the Use: box in the Content area.)
4. Add about 30 pixels worth of monochromatic noise to give the text some texture.
5. Apply Photoshop's Effects Chrome filter with Detail set to 10 and Smoothness to 0 to produce a swirling metallic look.
6. Create a new layer underneath the chrome lettering.
7. Choose the Linear Gradient tool, and select Chrome in the Gradient Options dialog box as the type of gradient.
8. Load the original text selection, and then place the cursor at the top of the letter T and drag down to fill the selection with the gradient.
9. Adjust the opacity of the gradient layer until you can see both the gradient and the chrome detailing of the letters.
10. Flatten the image and use Image | Adjust | Levels to lighten or darken the chromed letters to your preference. You should see something like Figure 8-11.

**Figure 8-11.** Chromed text

## Blocks of Ice

The same technique we used to create chromed text can carve letters from a block of ice.  Just follow these steps:

1. In a new, empty document, insert the word *Ice* with the Type Mask tool (or other text of your choosing).  I selected the font Schneidler because it has flowing curves and rounded serifs that already look as if they were molded from ice.
2. Fill the selection with a light blue tone.
3. Save the selection; then fill with random noise.  In this case, I used Photoshop's Film Grain filter with Grain set to 4 and Intensity set to 10.
4. Next, duplicate the current layer and, working with the copy, apply the Chrome filter, with Detail set to 10 and Smoothness to 0.
5. Finally, outline the letters with Edit:Stroke, set at 100 percent. Make sure black is the current foreground color.
6. Now, set the Opacity for the chromed layer to about 60 percent or any other blend that gives you the icy texture you like.
7. I added Eye Candy's Water Drops filter, using the built-in Many preset from the drop-down list at the right center of the dialog box.
8. Then, I duplicated the text layer, applied Ulead Text Effect's Snow filter, loaded the text selection I saved in Step 3, and deleted everything inside it on the Snow filter layer.  That left only the frosty ice hanging down around the letters.
9. If you really want to overdo it, make a rough selection around the tops of the letters and apply the Snow filter one more time.
10. Flatten the image, which will look something like the two versions shown in Figure 8-12.

## Stencil

A stencil effect can be used as a "fake" transparent graphic to blend in with your Web page's plain colored background.  Simply make the text described in the following set of instructions on a background that matches that of your Web page.  Follow these simple steps for an effective stencil-style look.  I'll give you three different methods to choose from.

1. Enter the text of your choice (I used the word *Stencil*) in a suitable font using the Type Mask tool.  I found Lithos to be the perfect choice, because it already includes some odd angles for its strokes.
2. Save the selection.
3. Now create the stenciled text using one of these three methods:

**Figure 8-12.** Snowy text

- Use a drop shadow filter, such as Eye Candy's Drop Shadow, and an offset (or Distance, in Eye Candy's case) of 0.
- Feather the selection using a value of around 8 pixels, and then fill it with black. Reload the original selection and cut out everything inside it, leaving only the stencil.
- For a more random, organic look, invert the selection and then spray around the outside with the Spray Can tool. You can vary the darkness of the overspray just by holding the tool in one position longer before moving on.

The three techniques are shown in Figure 8-13.

## Global Results

You've already seen how rounded or spherical buttons can add a desirable 3D effect to a Web page. You can also apply this three-dimensional quality to text, making the type appear to be printed on or wrapped around a globe. This next project will show you how.

1. Add your text to a transparent layer of a new image. I used a 600 x 600-pixel RGB image to leave plenty of room to experiment. I made the text about half the width of the image.
2. Fill the text with black, and then copy it, and paste the duplicate into a new layer.

3. Fill the duplicate with a light color, such as yellow. Then place it below and offset slightly from the original version to produce a 3D effect, as shown in Figure 8-14.

4. Choose Layer | Merge Visible to combine the two text layers.

5. On a new layer, create a perfectly circular selection. Choose the elliptical marquee tool. (Alt/Option-click on the rectangular marquee tool if it is showing.) Hold down the Alt/Option and Shift keys while you drag to create a perfect circle.

6. With the Marquee tool active, move the selection so the text is centered inside it.

7. Fill the selection with a color. We chose blue. Make sure this layer is located below the text layer in the Layers palette.

8. Using the Brush tool with a small hard-edged brush, create latitude lines on the disk, as shown in Figure 8-15.

9. Use Layer | Merge Visible again to combine the layers you've produced so far.

10. Apply Photoshop's Spherize filter or, if you have Kai's Power Tools, the Glass Lens filter set to Soft.

11. Use Image | Adjust | Levels or Brightness/Contrast to give your image a little extra snap. The final result is shown in Figure 8-16.

**Figure 8-13.** Three techniques for producing stencil effects

**Figure 8-14.**  Basic 3D text

**Figure 8-15.**  Text on globe

**Figure 8-16.** Spherized global text

## Making the Gradient

Here's a slick effect you can achieve using gradients such as the ones
you can produce with KPT Gradient Designer. Follow these steps to create an impressive corporate logo for your page.

1. Enter the text into a new file. I used the name of Macronesia International, the world's second-largest largest fictitious producer of
   computer hardware, software, and limpware. I selected the Peig-
   not font, and centered it.
2. Fill the text with a linear gradient, starting with white at the left and
   black at the right. You can also use another combination of light
   or dark colors.
3. Copy the text and paste down into a new layer, and fill the second copy
   with the same gradient, going the opposite direction.
4. With both layers visible, use the cursor arrow keys to move the second
   copy up and to the right by a few pixels, until you get the three-
   dimensional effect shown in Figure 8-17. Note that because the
   gradients are the opposite of one another, the light letters have
   dark drop shadows, and the dark letters have light drop shadows.
5. Create another layer below the text layer and fill it with a contrasting radial gradient, bursting out from the center to dark edges. I used
   shades of red.

**Figure 8-17.** Dueling gradients

6. Apply the Lens Flare filter to the center of this layer to backlight the text. I used the 105mm Lens setting and a Brightness level of 125 percent.
7. Adjust the opacity of the individual layers to your taste if necessary; then flatten the image. The final result is shown in Figure 8-18.

## 3D Text

Would you like some honest-to-goodness 3D text—the kind that requires 3D glasses to view? If you can convince visitors to your site to don red and blue glasses when viewing your special 3D pages, you can create this effect easily. Just follow these directions.

1. Create some text, fill it with a medium color, and then copy, paste into a new layer, and fill the copy with a dark color. Offset the two and flatten the image to end up with medium text displayed with a hard-edged drop shadow, as shown in Figure 8-19.
2. Save the file under a name of your choice. Do not save it again until we are finished. We need a copy of the original, unaltered text.
3. In the Channels palette, turn off all the channels except for Red.
4. Use Filter | Other | Offset to  move the red channel (only) a precise amount. Enter -4 for both horizontal and vertical values. Check the Repeat Edge pixels box.

**Figure 8-18.** Glorious Macronesia International logo

**Figure 8-19.** Basic text

5. Now make the blue channel (only) visible and enter +4 for the horizontal and vertical values. You'll end up with a 3D image like the one shown in Figure 8-20.

## Dramatic Lighting

Don't be afraid to use strong illumination on your text to give it the 3D look and feel you want. This example uses Photoshop's Lighting Effects filter in a dramatic way. Here are some easy steps you can follow for similar results:

1. Create your text on a transparent layer.
2. Apply Photoshop's Lighting Effects filter. Adjust the coverage of the light as shown in Figure 8-21 so that the light covers only part of the text. I set the filter's Properties to Shiny and Plastic, and turned on texture mapping for the red channel, bumping the effect all the way up to mountainous.
3. You can use the text as is, as shown at top in Figure 8-22, or do as I did at the bottom of the figure and apply a reverse gradient and drop shadow. In this case, I used Photoshop 5's new Layer Effects drop shadow, but you can work with any of the drop shadow techniques described in this book.

**Figure 8-20.** 3D glasses required

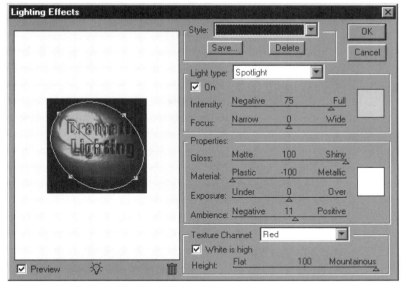

**Figure 8-21.** Set Lighting Effects to these parameters.

**Figure 8-22.** Two different effects

# ■ New Type Tools

One of the most dramatic changes in Photoshop 5 is the ability to edit text layers at will, up until the time you flatten the image. Photoshop users now have several ways to enter text into their images:

- As a Type Mask. In this mode, a selection is made in the shape of the text within the current layer. You can save the selection, fill it with a color, move the selection, feather it, or perform any operation you can apply to other kinds of selections. Because Type Mask doesn't create a new layer, it's a quick way of adding text to an existing layer if you know you won't want to be editing the text later on. I used the Type Mask tool frequently in this book, both for speed and to reduce the number of lengthy explanations I'd need otherwise to account for the differences between Photoshop 4 and Photoshop 5. Type Mask works the same in both versions. There is also a vertical Type Mask tool (marked with a downward pointing arrow on its icon) that allows you to create type turned 90 degrees without needing to rotate the selection manually.

- As a Type layer. In this Photoshop 5 mode, type is created in a separate layer that you can edit just by double-clicking the layer in the Layers Palette. You may change the font, size, or text itself. The text remains editable until you flatten the image or render it using the Layer | Type | Render Layer command. This mode also has a vertical type equivalent for producing rotated type. You can still edit the type in a horizontal orientation in the Type Tool dialog box, but view it onscreen in its rotated form. The Photoshop 5 Type Tool dialog box is shown in Figure 8-23.

Phototools provides similar enhancements to Photoshop 4 users plus additional capabilities that Photoshop 4 and 5 users will appreciate. PhotoTools has seven components, including PhotoBars (which allow you to add badly needed button bars to Photoshop), PhotoText (which upgrades the program for editable text), and the plug-in filters we have been using elsewhere in this book.

The PhotoBars tool allows you to put any Photoshop menu item on a button, and then dock the bars at an edge of the screen, or in a resizable floating palette. The enhancement even includes a SmartBar wizard that watches what you do and adds those commands.

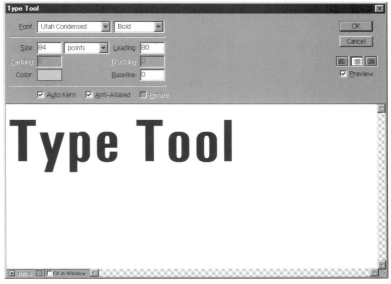

**Figure 8-23.** Photoshop 5 Type Tool dialog box

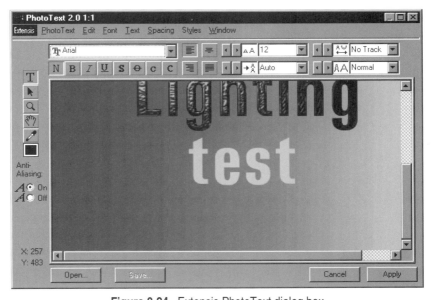

**Figure 8-24.** Extensis PhotoText dialog box

PhotoText goes well beyond the capabilities in the Photoshop 5 upgrade. Not only can you mix fonts, sizes, colors, and styles in a single block of text, but you have much more control over leading, kerning, tracking, and alignment. Particular text parameters can be saved as a style you can use over and over. The PhotoText dialog box is shown in Figure 8-24.

# ■ Moving On

There are other text effects elsewhere in this book, but I wanted to dedicate one full chapter to showing you the kinds of things you can do with fonts and plug-ins. In the next chapter, we're going to look at how you can optimize your Web graphics, with more detail on transparent and interleaved formats.

# chapter

# 9

# Optimizing Web Graphics

As Mark Twain never said, the difference between a good Web graphic and a great on-line image is like the difference between a lightning bug and lightning. You've learned how to create eye-catching buttons, backgrounds, rules, and other objects in the first eight chapters of this book. Now I'm going to show you how to take your images to the next level: optimizing them for Web display.

## ■ In This Chapter

- Choosing the Right Format
- Indexed Color
- Examples
- Minimizing Colors
- Resizing Images
- Resizing Tips
- Interpolation
- Balancing Color

We've touched on some of these topics earlier in the book, but we'll be looking at all four processes in a lot more detail in this chapter as we discover how plug-ins can help ensure the best results for graphics that attract rather than distract.

# ■ Choosing the Right Format

I explained the differences between GIF and JPEG formats in Chapter 4, but provided only a few guidelines to use in deciding which format is better for your image. I'm going to examine each of the dominant Web file formats and give you the information you need to make the best decision every time.

## GIF

The World Wide Web, or something much like it, was only a dream when I first ventured on-line in 1981. Those of us who used The Source or CompuServe to send email, engage in on-line chats, or download files were immersed in a nongraphical text-based environment without the images and hyperlinks that have made the Web so robust. Given the 300-bps speed of modems in those days—which produced horizontal scrolling as each line of text appeared on the screen character by character—and the lack of high-resolution images on computers of the time, on-line graphics were almost impossible.

By the late 1980s, however, Macs and PCs could handle images, while faster modems that could download them in a reasonable period of time became available. In response, CompuServe introduced the Graphic Interchange Format (GIF), which quickly became a de facto standard because the files were relatively small and viewers for both PCs and Macintoshes were available.

GIF uses a form of data compression first described by Abraham Lempel and Jacob Ziv in 1977 and refined by Terry Welch in 1984. This LZW compression (named after its originators' initials) reduces file size by replacing long strings of picture information with shorter numbers found in a data "dictionary." No image information is lost; the file becomes smaller thanks to these "abbreviations" created on the fly, which can always be expanded to produce a perfect copy of the original. However, the system supports only 256 colors, so any image that contains more than 256 tones must be converted for display with a reduced-size palette.

Although GIF is available in both GIF87a and GIF89a formats, the more recent GIF89a version (which supports transparency, interlacing, and animation) is the only GIF format you should consider using, as virtually all graphics-capable browsers now in use support these variations:

- Transparency: One color (and only one) is selected as the transparent color, and the browser will automatically display the background color or image through it. Your image should have a hard edge around the perimeter to be used as a transparent GIF. Feathering and anti-aliasing will show up as a white halo.

- Interlacing: With an interlaced GIF, the browser will display sets of alternating lines, or fields, so the image appears first in a rough rendition, and then is shown gradually more sharply as the missing lines are filled in. Interlaced GIFs provide your visitor with a preview of the image that's coming (hopefully in just a few seconds if you've made it a reasonable size). This kind of GIF is most useful only if visitors can get helpful information from the partial image; if they must wait until the entire GIF is downloaded to view it—as when the GIF contains text information—interlaced GIFs save no time and can be frustrating to wait for.

- Animation: Animated GIFs are special GIFs containing multiple images as individual frames. The browser will display each frame in succession using the interval you specified when you created the GIF (usually through a plug-in or stand-alone program unless you have an image editor that can create animated GIFs internally).

Because of the way GIF compression works, certain kinds of images can be squeezed down more efficiently than others. The GIF version of LZW encoding examines an image line by line, looking for repeating patterns of pixels. So, an image that contains many regular horizontal lines, like the one at left in Figure 9-1, would compress very well. A few entries in the file's data dictionary would define all the lines in the image, so the file could be compressed down to a few pointers to those entries. On the other hand, an image with vertical lines or irregular image areas, like the one at right, would require a much larger data dictionary to accommodate all the variations.

In addition, you may define how many different colors are included in a GIF file, from as few as 2 up to the maximum of 256. Given the same basic image, the one represented in fewer colors will be smaller. So, a GIF measuring 256 x 256 pixels could be much larger or much smaller than a JPEG image of the same size, depending on the content and number of colors used.

The GIF format is great for images with 256 or fewer colors and may be your only choice if you require transparency and animation—at least until the PNG (portable net graphics) format becomes more widely supported.

**Figure 9-1.** GIF compresses images with horizontal lines better than other types.

## JPEG

JPEG was developed by the Joint Photographic Experts Group, a consortium of organizations with interests in the photography and imaging industries. JPEG was designed to use a more advanced encoding system than GIF, using three different algorithms: a numeric compression scheme something like the LZW code used in GIF; a quantization routine, in which similar colors are grouped together; and a process called discrete cosine transformation, which involves some fancy math mumbo jumbo.

The key to the success of JPEG is the fact that our eyes don't really notice all the details in images, but, rather, tend to blend pixels into recognizable form. As a result, images can be created that discard some information, making the file much smaller, but still allowing a decent quality graphic. Figure 9-2 shows a pixelated image; if you squint, you'll have no trouble making out the original graphic, despite the minimal resolution of this blocky version.

A similar process happens when an image is JPEG-encoded. Figure 9-3 shows a small image, roughly 190 x 190 pixels in its original TIF format at left, and, at right, after it has been saved as a JPEG using the maximum compression ratio. You probably wouldn't want to use such extreme compression for a Web graphic in which the details were impor-

**Figure 9-2.** Even pixelated images are recognizable.

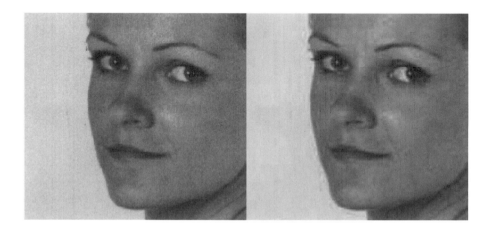

**Figure 9-3.** TIFF (left) and JPEG (right) versions of the same image

tant, but you can see that the image is still quite recognizable. Yet, the TIFF file takes up five times as much disk space—35K versus 7K for the JPEG image.

Figure 9-4 shows clearly what happened during the compression process. The enlargement at left shows the original image. The square dots are actual image pixels of this 100-dpi grayscale image. Each pixel can contain any of 256 different values. (If we'd used a color picture, the pixel could be any of 16.7 million different colors.)

At right, the image has been squeezed using JPEG compression. You can see that the image has been divided into blocks of 64 pixels. Pixels that are similar in tone to those around them are discarded and represented by a tone even closer to that of its neighbors. The result is an image that, on close examination, is blocky and lower in contrast— and you'll recall that contrast between pixels translates into apparent sharpness. A JPEG image may appear less sharp than an original, but the more even tones can be compressed much, much more efficiently— often 20:1 or more, depending on the content.

Because pixel information is discarded, JPEG is called a lossy compression scheme. You can specify how much data is thrown out by the algorithm, giving you control over both the file size and quality of the image. This ability to include any of 16.7 million different colors and also custom-tailor an image's size and sharpness based on the needs of

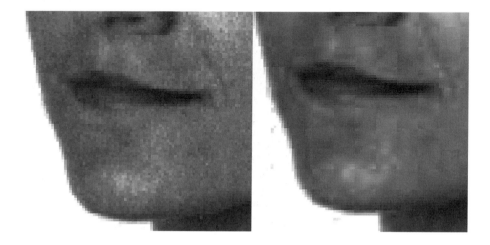

**Figure 9-4.** TIFF (left) and JPEG (right) enlargements

your Web page make JPEG a great tool for Internet images.  JPEG images are best suited for images that demand smoother gradations of color that GIF can provide and that don't require the transparency or animation features found in the GIF format.

# ■ Indexed Color

Now that you understand the differences between GIF and JPEG, we can look at methods for optimizing the quality of images in each format. We'll start with GIF and the subject of defining which colors will be used.

Converting to 256 tones or fewer is generally done through *indexing* or a *color look-up table* (CLUT).  The colors of the original image are mapped to an indexed palette or color look-up table, as shown in Figure 9-5.  A range of similar colors are all indexed to a particular tone in the palette, so that any image converted using that palette will represent any and all of those hues with the indexed color.  As you might imagine, with 16.7 million possible colors in a 24-bit color image, 256 tones must each go a long way.  Specifically, if an image contained one of each possible color (which is highly unlikely), each color in a 256-color palette would have to represent more than 65,000 different hues in the original!  Fortunately, nothing like this is required in the real world.

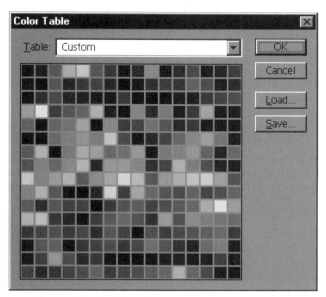

**Figure 9-5.** An indexed palette or color look-up table

Our eyes can't differentiate such fine gradations in tone in the first place. A color represented by values of 62 Red, 62 Green, and 114 Blue (a very deep blue) looks almost identical to any of the dozens of variations you'd get by modifying any or all of those values plus or minus five or so. I guarantee that you'd find it difficult to tell that blue from, say, 57 Red, 57 Green, 119 Blue.

More importantly, a given image won't (*can't*) contain anywhere near 16.7 million different colors. Think about it. A largish 256 x 256-pixel image contains a total of 65,536 different pixels. Even if each and every one were a different color (again, highly unlikely), no more than 65,536 colors would be required to represent them. In an average-sized 128 x 128-pixel graphic, each color in a 256-color palette would need to represent only 64 different hues and, as I've said, many of them will be so close in color that the substitution will be almost invisible to the eye.

The exception is for continous-tone color images that contain fine gradations of colors, say, a gradient from light blue to dark blue. In such cases, groups of adjoining colors will be lumped into a single entry in the indexed palette, causing a phenomenon known as banding, shown in Figure 9-6. Clearly, some images lend themselves to indexed color, while others do not. As you might expect, black-and-white photos do best of all. Monochrome image files by convention contain just 256 shades of gray so they can be represented quite accurately by a 256-color palette.

**Figure 9-6.** Banding

So, it is quite feasible to map dozens of different colors down to 256 or fewer—if your software is smart enough to choose the right set of colors that matches the most colors in your original image.  If a CLUT concentrates on too many reds, for example, there may not be enough tones left over to represent the blues in an image.

While Photoshop and other image editors have conversion facilities for reducing the number of colors to 256 or fewer, plug-ins, like the GIF SmartSaver we used in Chapter 4,  can help even more.  Let's look at Photoshop's own capabilities first.

## GIF89a Export Plug-In

Beginning with Photoshop 4, Adobe's program has had its own built-in GIF Export plug-in that automatically reduces images to 256 or fewer colors. (For Version 3, the plug-in was a separate module that could be downloaded and installed separately.)  We've already used it to create transparent GIFs, but a review is in order.

When you activate Photoshop's GIF plug-in, the dialog box shown in Figure 9-7 appears.  Your main control is the Palette drop-down list, which allows you to select either the operating system's own 256-color palette, an Adaptive palette (an array of the most frequently used colors in an image), or, if the image already contains 256 or fewer colors, an Exact palette, which will use all the colors currently in the graphic.

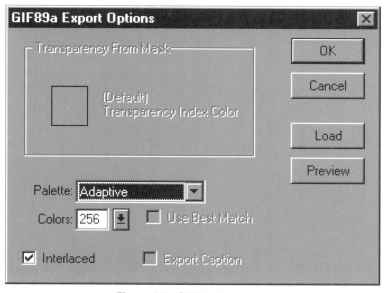

**Figure 9-7.** GIF89a dialog box.

You can also choose the number of colors—8, 16, 32, 64, 128, 255, or 256—from the Colors drop-down list.

Other buttons in this dialog box allow you to load a palette already stored on disk or view a preview of the image and the color look-up table that will result with the current settings. The preview is shown in Figure 9-8. You're not given a lot of flexibility with this plug-in, which is why it's almost always better to use a third party plug-in to reduce colors, or work with Photoshop's more versatile Mode facilities.

## Photoshop's Mode Facility

Using the Image | Mode | Indexed Color dialog box offers many more options, including the ability to define your own color look-up table. The basic dialog box looks like Figure 9-9. It includes a palette pull-down list like the GIF89a Export plug-in, but has some additional controls.

The Palette list has Adaptive, Exact, and System choices, just like the GIF export module, although the System selection is broken down into separate Macintosh and Windows systems palettes, since they differ. Some additional palettes are also available:

- **Web:** This selection uses the common palette of 216 colors that Web browsers can show on a system set for 256-color display. What happened to the extra 40 colors? Those hues are reserved by the operating system for showing menus, icons, scroll bars, and so on, leav-

**Figure 9-8.** GIF89a preview

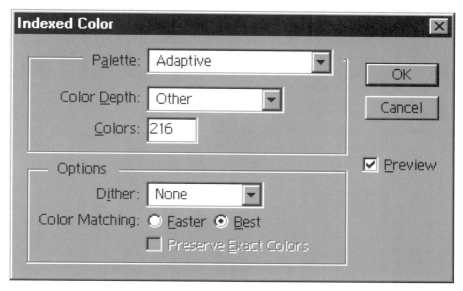

**Figure 9-9.** Indexed Color dialog box

ing just 216 for your graphics. Even if you expect that all visitors to
your site will have high-color displays (not a safe assumption, by
the   way), using only browser-safe colors can make it easier for the
browser to display all the images on your page with the colors you
intended. If several images on a page use different palettes, some
color shifts can occur as the browser attempts to display all of them.
With the Web palette, they'll all use the same set of colors.

- **Uniform:** This is a palette based on a uniform sampling of colors
  and usually not a good choice for Web graphics.
- **Previous:** This choice applies the last color look-up table used to
  the current image. You'd use this to apply a custom palette to several different images that will appear on the same page.
- **Custom:** This choice allows you to load a previously saved CLUT or
  create a new one with surprising ease. Figure 9-10 shows a typical
  color table. Note that there are many "wasted" dark colors at the
  tail end of the table. You can double-click any individual color to
  produce the Color Picker and then choose a color from that. Or, you
  can drag with the mouse to select the whole range of colors. In that
  case, Photoshop asks you to select starting and ending colors, and
  fills in the selected pixels with a gradient of tones between the two,
  generating a modified CLUT like the one shown in Figure 9-11.
  You could use this feature if an image has, say, a great many brown

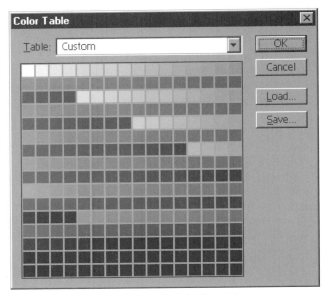

**Figure 9-10.** Typical color table

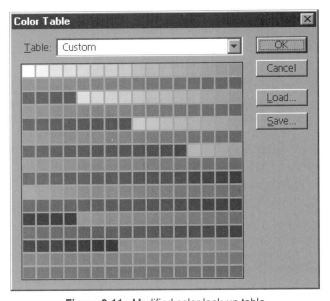

**Figure 9-11.** Modified color look-up table

tones and you want to provide plenty of colors in that range for the indexed palette.

- Other Options: You can choose color depth, from 3 to 8 bits per pixel (8 to 256 colors), but only if you're using the Adaptive palette. You may also select a dither pattern, as described in the following examples.

# ■ Examples

I converted a 24-bit color image. You can compare your own results with mine, although the different results you get with various options are obvious even in the grayscale versions on these pages.

## Web Palette

Figure 9-12 shows the original image at left, a yellow-violet-orange-blue gradient using Photoshop 5's new angle gradient tool. At right is the same image reduced to 216 colors with the Web palette option. Notice that the program has grouped similar colors together, representing them with a smaller number of hues. A pronounced banding effect is produced. However, we didn't use a process called dithering, which increases the number of apparent colors in an image.

**Figure 9-12.** Original image (left) and same image at 216 colors (right)

## Dithers

Dithering uses combinations of pixels in various colors to mimic the intermediate colors that result when you combine them. Although there are dozens of different dithering schemes, Photoshop offers just two of them. They are Pattern dither, which uses a halftone-like regular arrangement of dots, and Diffusion dither, which applies a more random arrangement that you might find more pleasing. Figure 9-13 shows both kinds of dither.

## Adaptive Palette

While the Web palette we just used was designed specifically for browsers, it doesn't always provide the best image on an 8-bit display when used with photographic images. The browser-safe colors often look good when used with logos, buttons, and other objects, particularly if they're displayed in a small size. However, for true continuous-tone images, the Adaptive Palette choice often produces superior results. It generates the colors used in an image by examining the colors in the original 24-bit version and weighting its selection based on the actual tones required for an image. The banding produced is usually much less than you get with the Web palette. In some cases, as you can see in Figure 9-14, it may be difficult to tell a 256-color Adaptive Palette image from the original full-color version.

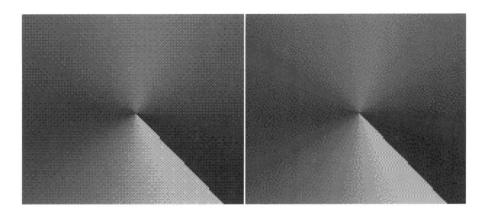

**Figure 9-13.** Pattern dither (left) and Diffusion dither (right)

**Figure 9-14.**  Adaptive Palette version

An image produced with the Adaptive Palette will always look better than any other 256- or 216-color image with a browser using a 24-bit display.  And, it is likely to look better on a 256-color display, as well. What's the deal here?  When you use the Adaptive Palette and a browser can display only 256 colors, it will generate a palette for your visitor on the fly.  Those colors may not match exactly the colors in the original image (even if they do look  good). If more than one image appears on a page and both use the Adaptive Palette, the browser's ad hoc palettes may not match each other very well, producing speckling or some other odd color effect in the visitor's browser.

The Web palette is "browser safe," while the Adaptive palette should look better with color photos.  Take your pick, depending on what is most important to you for a given graphic.

# ■ Minimizing Colors

Because GIF starts out as a lossless compression scheme, the only way to make a GIF file smaller is to intentionally discard some information. That's commonly done by reducing the number of colors in an image. When you're using the Adaptive palette with the Mode dialog box, or GIF89a Export plug-in, Photoshop gives you the option of selecting 128, 64, 32, 16,  and 8 colors.  In addition, you can type in another color value (say, 152) if you know an image has only that many colors.  Eliminating unneeded colors from the palette can make an image dramatically smaller and may not degrade your image too much. Figure 9-15 shows an image taken from a Spanish castle, originally in 24-bit color. However, the castle itself is mostly shades of brown and contains fewer than 256 colors even without any special techniques. Better yet, it can be reduced to even fewer hues without significantly affecting the image. At left, a version in 256-color mode at 300 x 450 pixels produced a 100K GIF file.

At right in the same figure is the castle in 3-bit, 8-color mode, a file that is 75% smaller at only 24K! In the full-size version you'd be hard-pressed to tell the difference. It takes a close-up look, as you can see in Figure 9-16, to detect the banding and other quality lost by dropping those extraneous colors. You probably won't have photographic images that lend themselves to color reduction as much as this one, but it's always worth a try when creating GIF files from other kinds of artwork. You may be surprised at how much space you save—and how much more quickly your files download.

# ■ Automating GIF and JPEG Optimization

You'll find a host of plug-ins and stand-alone programs to help you optimize GIF and JPEG images, beyond those we've already looked at in

**Figure 9-15.** Left, 256 colors; right, 8 colors for the same image

t

**Figure 9-16.** Losses through banding shown by comparing image at left, 256 colors, and at right, 8 colors for the same image

his book, such as Ulead's GIF and JPEG SmartSavers.  Here are brief descriptions of the best of these tools.

## HVS ColorGIF

This Photoshop-compatible plug-in for both Windows and Mac systems from Digital Frontier uses sophisticated algorithms to help you produce the smallest possible GIFs, with or without dithering.  HVS Color selects and assigns colors to a special adaptive palette, and can create regions of color without dithering that nevertheless have smooth color gradations.  This system allows the GIF format's LZW compression scheme to do a better job than standard GIF of reducing the size of the data. And the images look better, because pure color looks cleaner and doesn't have the characteristic graininess of dithered images.

Unlike color reduction systems that assign colors based only on how frequently they appear in an image, HVS ColorGIF takes into account the fact that the human eye cannot distinguish between extremely dark or light colors—say, values below 16 or above 240.  Instead of assigning precious 8-bit tones to shades of black or white, the plug-in reallocates these values to colors that we can see.  HVS Color GIF includes features that provide

- Smooth operation with Photoshop Action-based batch processing.
- The ability to process any combination of Layers or a selected portion of an image.
- Immediate previews showing image quality, GIF size, and download time estimates.
- Facility for creating palettes usable with multiple images.
- Optimization of the CLUTs of existing GIFs.
- Control over transparency, including the ability to specify several colors as transparent. The colors are merged into the single color required for transparent GIFs.
- Size and download time estimate with each change of settings.

## HVS JPEG

Digital Frontier also offers HVS JPEG, which helps generate the best-looking JPEG images we've seen. This plug-in has 100 different quality/compression ratios, or you can use the familiar settings such as Low, Medium, High, and Maximum quality. You get control of detail and strength of edge detail, as well as optimized tables for several different image types, such as portraits and textures. The plug-in can also save progressive JPEGs for applications—including most recent Web browsers—that can support them.

## PhotoGIF/ProJPEG/ColorSafe

This trio of plug-ins from BoxTop Software intelligently reduce the number of colors in an image, with a facility to adjust dithering incrementally so you can reduce banding and soften edges without producing unwanted artifacts in areas of flat color. PhotoGIF and ProJPEG provide preview windows and use sliders to help you optimize an image quickly. ColorSafe is a more advanced product that allows manipulating a variety of custom palettes in addition to a 216-color browser-safe version.

## smartGIF

SiteJazz's smartGIF is an unusual tool that, in addition to its palette manipulation capabilities, helps you build graphic layouts using multiple GIFs. With smartGIF you can divide an open image into sections and export each section as an individual GIF files each with customized palette type, dithering, exact numbers of colors you specify, transparency color, interlacing, and more. It offers real time previews of file size and image quality, and can combine palettes from several images so all will look good when displayed on the same page.

Once you've exported sections of a GIF as individual files, you can use HTML tables to array them in a layout of your choice. Each image can link to a different object on your site, making this an easy way to create an image map without the bother of creating client-side or server-side image map files.

# Resizing Images

One step in optimizing images may be to resize them from their current dimensions. There are several instances where you'll need to resize images:

- When you want a smaller version to use as a thumbnail, say, of a photograph. You can include HTML code on a Web page to show an image in a smaller size, but the visitor must download the full-size image before this thumbnail can be created. A better solution is to create an actual thumbnail image through resizing, and allow display of the original through an HTML link.
- When you need a smaller version to preserve a consistent theme or look. You might, for example, have a large button for main choices and a smaller version for subsidiary selections on a Web page. Again, browsers can display reduced-size versions, but if you want to customize your smaller buttons, you'll have to resize them from the original. Figure 9-17 shows some buttons created in this way.
- When you have an original image that is larger than you need for your Web page.
- When it is easier to work with a larger image, and then reduce it to

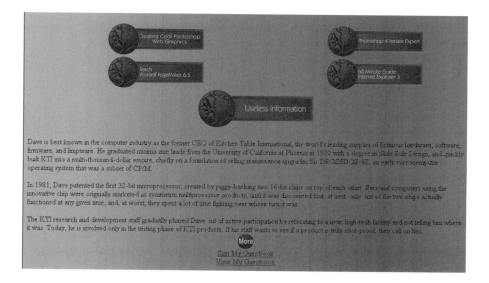

**Figure 9-17.** Resized buttons

the size you need. Some filters don't operate well on small areas of an image. By working with a larger size, you get better control over the effect and can reduce the image when finished.

# ■ Resizing Tips

Here are some tips that will help you resize images effectively:
- If you don't know exactly what size your finished object will need to be, create it in a larger size and then reduce.
- Save a copy of the original image in case you need to resize again later. You'll always get the best results resizing an original, rather than attempting to resize an image that has already been resized once. Enlarging an object that has been reduced in size will produce especially poor results, as you can see in Figure 9-18.
- Preview your Web pages at both 1024 x 768 and 640 x 480 resolutions so you have an idea of what size is best for a particular object. Don't make them so small that they can't be viewed at higher resolutions or so large that they hog the screen at lower settings.
- If possible, use factors of 2 when resizing images. Objects will always look better at 50, 25, 200 and 400% than at 33, 17.2 or 175%.
- If you need to resize a GIF image, convert it to JPEG first, resize, and then export as a GIF. Most image editors do a rotten job resizing GIFs or any 256-color image for that matter.

# ■ Interpolation

Each time you resize an image or change the resolution of an image, even if the size remains the same, your image editor must create new pixels or throw some away, using a process called interpolation. In Photoshop, you may choose the mathematical algorithms used to calculate the new pixels. Your three choices are
- **Nearest Neighbor** With this method, Photoshop adds pixels by copying from the nearest pixel next to the position where the new

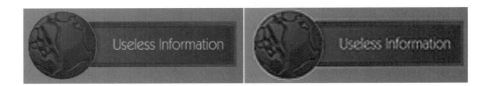

**Figure 9-18.** Left, original image; right, reduced image enlarged to original size again

**Color 33.** Original image (top), Watercolor (center), and Angled Strokes (bottom)

**Color 34.** Fresco and Spatter filters

**Color 35.** Photoshop's Ink Outlines filter produces a fine-art look.

**Color 36.** Cutout, Mosaic Tiles, and Poster Edges filters

**Color 37.** Diffuse Glow is a great filter for creating a romantic look.

**Color 38.** Paint Alchemy offers some great brushstroke tools.

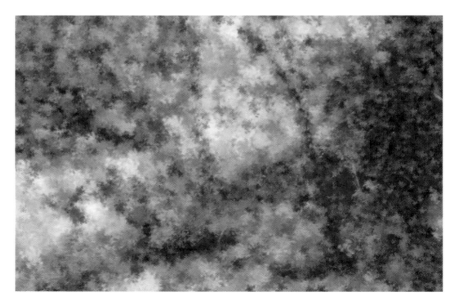

**Color 39.** A sharp photo can be changed into an impressionistic background using techniques described in Chapter 11.

**Color 40.** PhotoText preview window, from Chapter 12

**Color 41.** Xaos Tools' Terrazzo filter creates kaleidoscopic effects.

**Color 42.** This amazingly realistic effect was produced by selecting different portions of the house, and then applying Eye Candy's Fire filter. Some areas were blacked out to simulate soot.

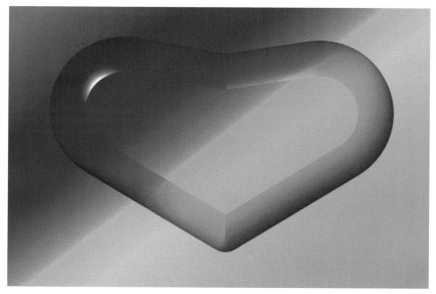

**Color 43.** Extensis's PhotoButton plug-in can generate a variety of effects.

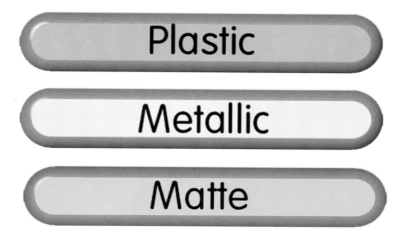

**Color 44.** Some subtle differences in surface texture

**Color 45.** KPT Spheroid Designer, Glass Lens and PhotoBevel
were combined to produce this effect.

**Color 46.** Copper gradient, enhanced with Eye Candy's Glass filter (top) and Outer Bevel (bottom)

**Color 47.** Instructions for creating this text can be found in Chapter 13.

one will go (when enlarging an image or increasing resolution) or by determining the value of a pixel that will replace others (when reducing an image or its resolution). On very slow computers (such as older 486 Windows systems or 680x0-based Macs), this faster system can speed up the process significantly. However, it works best with line art rather than continuous-tone images because the process doesn't take much account of the fine gradations that occur in tonal transitions.

- **Bilinear** This method bases its calculations on the values of the pixels above, below, and to either side of the new or replacement pixel. While not as fast as Nearest Neighbor, it produces better quality.

- **Bicubic** This interpolation method uses sophisticated algorithms to calculate a new pixel based on surrounding pixels. Unless you have a very slow computer, this choice should be your default, as it produces much finer gradations and significantly higher quality than the other interpolation methods. Actually, even people who own slowpokes are better off using bicubic interpolation and just scheduling a coffee break during resampling. Figure 9-19 shows an image resampled using each of these three methods.

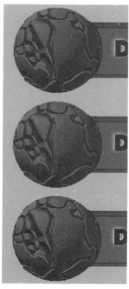

**Figure 9-19.** Image resampled using (top to bottom) Nearest Neighbor, Bilinear, and Bicubic interpolation methods

# ■ Balancing Color

Color balance is the relationship between the three colors used to produce your image: red, green, and blue. You need to worry only about three different factors: how much red, green, and blue are in an image; the saturation of each color (that is, how much of the hue is composed of the pure color itself, and how much is diluted by a neutral color, such as white or black); the brightness and contrast of the image (the relative lightness/darkness of each color and the number of different tones available).

Bad color can be caused by everything from incorrect or mixed light sources when the original photo was taken on film or digitally, to bad photofinishing and faded prints. Unfortunately, for Web applications, optimal color is difficult to achieve because colors will vary from browser to browser, from Mac to PC platforms, between different users, or even when palettes are created on the fly when 24-bit color is shown on a display set for 256 hues. The best you can hope for is to balance color so it looks good on your properly calibrated system, and then trust that your visitors are configured reasonably well, too.

Some images can't be corrected. *Removing* one color, or *changing* some colors to another color doesn't add any color to your image. Either way, you're taking color out. So, if you have an image that is hopelessly and overpoweringly green, you're out of luck. When you remove all the green, there may be no color left behind. Or, you can add magenta until your subject's face turns blue, and all you'll end up with is a darker photo. You must start with a reasonable image; color correction is better suited for fine-tuning than for major overhaul.

In addition to plug-ins like those discussed later in this chapter, your choices for balancing color are these:

- Your image's color balance controls. This method is oriented most toward brute force and may be a little complicated for the neophyte. Depending on your particular software, you may have to hunt to find a set of sliders that can be used to adjust all colors for an entire image. They usually let you adjust the proportions of a particular color, from 0 to 100 percent. In the case of Photoshop, you can either add one color or subtract its two component colors. If you want to add pure red (or green or blue), you can move the relevant control to the right. If your needs lean a little more toward one of the component colors than the other, move those sliders to the left, instead. For example, you can remove red in one of two ways: by adding cyan (thereby subtracting red) or by adding green and blue (thereby subtracting magenta and yellow).

- You can also color correct an image using the Hue/Saturation/Lightness or (Brightness) controls found in most image editors. The advantage of correcting color this way is that you can change the saturation of individual colors or of all the colors in an image without modifying the hue or lightness/darkness of those colors. The color balance method changes only the relationships between the colors.

- Advanced workers can really fine-tune color using their image editor's Curves command. You'll need to have a deep understanding of how color works to use this sophisticated method; it's doubtful if Web images require such a fine degree of control, anyway.

- Use Variations. You can play with the color balance of an image for hours at a time, never quite achieving what you are looking for. There's no guarantee that, after a lot of work, you might decide that an earlier version really did look better after all. Image editors are jumping on the "color ring around" or "variations" bandwagon. In this mode, shown in Figure 9-20, the software itself generates sev-

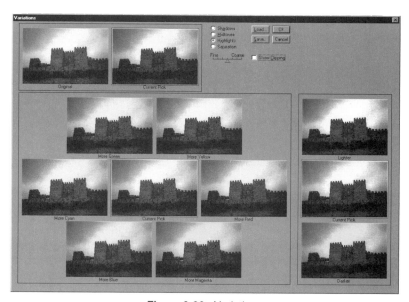

**Figure 9-20.** Variations

eral versions of an image, arranged in a circle or other array so you can view a small copy of each one and compare them. Photoshop's Variations mode is especially useful, but you can purchase plug-ins like Vivid Detail's Test Strip (for Macs only) that provide even finer control over your color comparisons.

Keep in mind that if you switch back and forth between RGB and CMYK, your colors can change. There are colors that can be represented by the RGB model that can't be duplicated in the CMYK model (and vice versa), so anytime you switch between the two, you run the risk of losing some colors. It's especially deadly to change from one model to the other, and then back to the original. Photoshop 3.0 added a preview mode that lets you view CMYK color schemes without actually changing the file's content, so you can return to RGB with your colors intact.

## Extensis Intellihance

If you're looking for a plug-in solution to image correction, Extensis has the answer for you. Intellihance, shown in Figure 9-21, is smart enough to turn most correction steps into a single-click operation.

It can remove halftone screens from images that have already been printed; delete color casts; remove dust and artifacts; enhance sharpness; and adjust brightness, contrast, or saturation automatically.

**Figure 9-21.** Extensis Intellihance dialog box

You can use Intellihance's default settings or establish your own preferences. With a single mouse click, you can toggle between the original image and enhanced version in the same zoomable preview image.

The same settings can be applied to multiple images, so you can process entire batches quickly.

## ■ Moving On

You don't have to be a programmer to create your own custom filters, presets, and effects. The next chapter will show you how to create your own filter factory with filters you can stockpile and share.

chapter
# 10

# Designing Your Own Filters

If none of the hundreds of filters available from Adobe and third parties suit your needs, you can create your own. You don't need to be a programming wizard with access to Adobe's plug-in software developer kit to create customized filters, either. Your favorite image editor already has three tools built in that anyone with a willingness to experiment can use productively.

You've probably used one of the three tools—presets, custom filters, and displacement maps—already. The presets capabilities found in Kai's Power Tools and other third-party filters are a quick way of creating customized filters you can reuse at any time. The KPT Gradient and Spheroid Designers, Texture Explorer, and Interform all are furnished with hundreds of presets and let you save your own. Eye Candy and Extensis Photo Tools filters also allow saving settings. Because the settings files are in standard formats readable by other copies of the same product, you can store your custom filters on disk and share them with colleagues who have the same plug-ins.

Custom filters allow you to enter your own parameters for contrast-altering filters, making it simple to create posterization, embossing, or colorizing effects on your own. The Displace filter can be used with maps you create for eye-catching, repeatable effects. Although workers who understand the math behind image processing can use any of these tools to create specific looks on demand, you can get good results just playing with the facilities.

Just be prepared to tell your colleagues, "I meant to do that!" when a happy accident occurs. While these effects can be a little unpredictable when applied to varying images, you'll soon learn how to create the sort of look you're searching for with only a little trial and few errors.

# ■ In This Chapter

- Working with Presets
- What are Convolutions?
- Using the Custom Filter
- Working with Displacement Maps
- Achieving Predictable results

# ■ Working with Presets

The folks at MetaCreations probably created those great presets the same way you might: a software designer sat down with Kai's Power Tools and played with various settings until something cool happened worth saving on disk for posterity. Spheroid Designer and Texture Explorer, in particular, lend themselves to this approach with their mutation buttons that allow creating random variations using one or more parameters you choose such as color, blending, rotation, or scale. A few clicks can generate hundreds of different effects. Even with such a wide variety of effects at your fingertips, you'll often want to save a particular setting for reuse later. For example, you might want to use a particular texture as part of a theme on your Web page, and would need to come back to it to create a new object. Without presets, you'd find it difficult to reproduce a particular effect once you'd exited your image editor.

# ■ KPT Presets

You can access the Presets menu via a downward-pointing triangle at the bottom of the plug-in's dialog box. A graphical preview window or text listing of the available presets, like the one shown in Figure 10-1, will pop up.

The text descriptions summarize what the designer of that preset thought the effect looked like. You may not agree, but the names—like Racing Grapes or Shredded Bubbles—are always easy to remember. If you need a particular preset and you know its name, the text listing is handy and fast. However, if you're browsing for an effect and don't know exactly what you want, the graphical presets display, like the one shown in Figure 10-2, is preferred. To scroll through this display, just

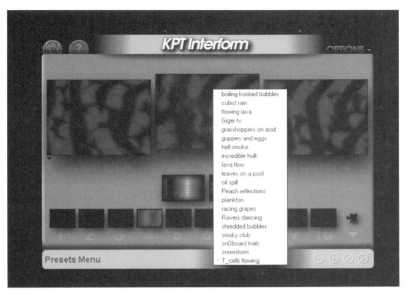

**Figure 10-1.** Text listing of presets

**Figure 10-2.** Graphical presets

slide the mouse up or down. Hold down the shift key to speed up the display of the presets. As you pass the cursor over a preset, its name will appear in the status area at the bottom left of the dialog box.

To select a preset, just click on its text name or image. Normally, you must hold down the mouse button to keep the presets visible on the screen, but if you hold down the shift key while you click the presets menu, the listings will remain until you click on a preset or anywhere else in the preset window.

For the plug-ins like Gradient and Spheroid Designers or Texture Explorer that have graphical displays, you can choose from a text list instead by clicking the circled minus sign at the bottom right of the dialog box. This is the Preset Manager, shown in Figure 10-3, and can be used to choose a preset, remove a preset, load a new set of presets, or save the presets that are currently active onto your hard disk. To move quickly to the preset you are looking for, click anywhere in the listing with the cursor, and then type in the first letter of its name; the Preset Manager will jump to the first preset beginning with that letter.

To add an effect to your current set of presets, click the circled plus sign at lower right of the dialog box. You'll be invited to type in a descriptive name. Be careful, however! Kai's Power Tools does absolutely nothing to prevent you from applying a name that is already in use. It will blithely apply the new name and deposit the preset in the alpha-

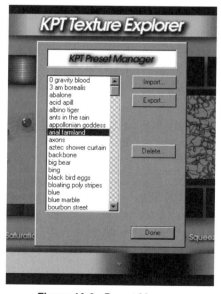

**Figure 10-3.** Preset Manager

betical text listing right next to the original.

Spheroid Designer has an additional kind of preset, a shortcut called memory dots in the upper right corner, first introduced with KPT Convolver (an earlier MetaCreations plug-in that's useful for fine-tuning effects if you can find a copy). The nine memory dots can be used to recall any setting just by clicking them. Click on any dark brown, unused memory dot to load the current settings into that memory dot. The dot will light up, changing to a glowing light brown. Clicking a lit memory dot resets your preview to the settings in use when the memory dot was originally set. To erase a memory dot, hold down the Option/Alt key and click it. Figure 10-4 shows a set of memory dots.

# ■ Other Presets and Capabilities

Most other plug-ins have their own options for saving settings or presets. With Eye Candy, you'll want to click the icon that looks like a writing pencil, as shown at center right in Figure 10-5, to pop up the settings saving dialog box. Click the other pencil to load settings.

Extensis's PhotoTools plug-ins include a Save button at the lower left corner of the dialog box, as you can see in Figure 10-6. You might have to hunt to find the Save button within other packages, but they're usually there somewhere. Human Software's Squizz includes a handy icon in the middle right of the screen, as shown in Figure 10-7.

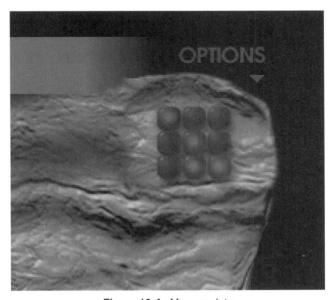

**Figure 10-4.** Memory dots

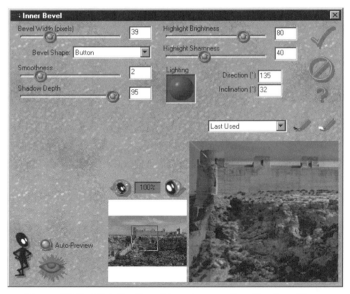

**Figure 10-5.** Click the Pencil icon to save Eye Candy settings.

**Figure 10-6.** PhotoTools filters include a Save button.

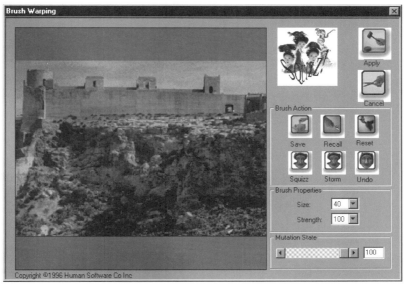

**Figure 10-7.** Save Squizz settings, too.

Although Photoshop's Actions' macro capabilities and the add-on product KPT Actions are neither plug-ins nor presets, they too can help you store customized filter effects by recording or playing back predefined lists of steps carried out using filters and other tools. Once you've captured an Action, you can apply it to any image later on just by running the macro another time. Photoshop allows you to store and share Actions just as you do filter presets.

# ■ **What Are Convolutions?**

A convolution is a series of mathematical operations performed on all the pixels in an image or selection. The math is a bit twisted or convoluted because the formulae are applied to one pixel based on the values of the pixels around it, which are themselves processed in turn. So, while the pixel at coordinates 1,1 (upper left and corner) may be brightened or darkened depending on the values of its neighbors (1,2 to the right, 2,1 below it, and 2,2 diagonally), its new value may be used to determine the modifications to the pixel at 1,2 when it's that pixel's turn to be convoluted. Is this confusing or what?

The operations needed to perform a particular effect are arranged in a matrix called a kernel, with the pixel being abused represented as a box in the center of the matrix, and the pixels surrounding it represented by boxes of their own. Numbers placed in the boxes determine

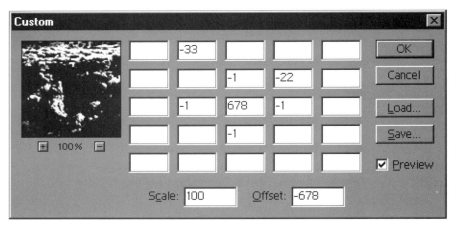

**Figure 10-8.** Sample convolution kernel

what happens to the poor center pixel. Figure 10-8—showing an example of a convolution kernel—just happens to represent the Photoshop Custom filter's dialog box.

If you'll look closely at the boxes in Figure 10-8, you'll see that there are various positive and negative numbers, which are used at processing time to change the value of the pixel in the center.

There are several kinds of kernels, such as Spatial and Color kernels, each relating to a particular property of your image. Filters that can work with these are able to modify both the image hue, saturation, and brightness as well as the apparent contrast between pixels, along with their positions.

The Custom filter happens to work with the brightness values of the pixels in relation to each other, so most of the effects you can generate with it represent things affected by brightness: contrast, sharpness (which is related to the contrast between adjacent pixels), and 3D effects, such as embossing (created by lightening or darkening certain pixels to create shadows and ridges.)

# ◼ Using the Custom Filter

To use the Custom filter, you'll need to find it in the Filters | Other menu. The dialog box in Figure 10-8 pops up, and contains some elements you are familiar with, such as the preview window at left with its plus and minus zoom buttons. At right, you'll also find the checkbox to turn previews on and off plus several buttons that let you save Custom filter presets that you want to reuse, or load previously saved settings.

It's those other parts of the dialog box that are confusing you, right? Here are a few hints:

- The center box represents the pixel being evaluated. You can type a number from 999 to -999 to multiply (lighten) or demultiply (darken) the pixel.
- All the adjacent boxes represent pixels in adjacent positions. You may type in numbers that will be used to multiply the brightness of the pixel in that position.

Figure 10-9 shows another kernel. In this kernel, the center pixel of each convolution will be multiplied by 6 to brighten it. The pixels to the left, to the right, above, and below the victim pixel will be darkened by a factor of -1. This has the effect of making the center pixel brighter than those that surround it.

Won't everything cancel out when the algorithm moves on to the next pixel? No, because the new pixel will already have been darkened by the convolution of its neighbor. In practice, you'll get some interesting effects, which you can already see in the preview window.

There are two other boxes in the dialog, labeled Scale and Offset. The value typed in Scale is used to divide the sum of the brightness values of the pixels included in the convolution. The value entered in the Offset box will be added to the results of the scale calculation. If you're a normal person, you're probably getting an uneasy feeling about now.

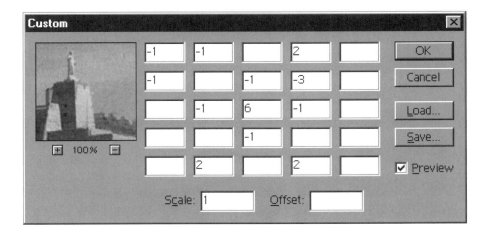

**Figure 10-9.** Sample kernel

Since you've studied math, maybe even calculus, everything I've said so far makes perfect sense to you. But what does it *mean*?

Here's the good news: You don't have to know what it means. Because one thing you certainly will not be doing is sitting down and trying to figure out how to multiply or divide pixel brightness values in order to achieve special effects. To use the Custom filter, all you really need to do is type in values into the available boxes and see what they do. Add a 1 here, a 6 there, maybe a 666 for the heck of it.

You'll see a small-scale glimpse of what's going on in the Preview window, plus a full view of the effect in your main image window. If you position the Custom dialog box off to one side, you can view your entire image and the dialog box at the same time.

That's right, all you need to do to have fun is just play around. If you get an effect you like, click on the Save button and choose a name that will help you remember what the effect did.

Custom filters that you create will vary in their effect quite sharply depending on the image that you apply them to. While a filter that decreases contrast or enhances edges will perform essentially a similar function on all the images you try, the effects may be drastically different, because the new image already had lower contrast or fewer sharp edges than the picture you used to create the filter. This is true for all filters, of course, but you can avoid some disappointment if you realize this up front.

Because Custom filters look different with different images, you may find that you use this plug-in most often to create a customized, one-off filter effect for a particular image. That will be the case after you've developed a bit of familiarity with what happens when you type figures into the kernel's matrix. You'll find yourself pulling down the Custom filter, typing in a few numbers, tweaking a bit more, and then clicking OK when you're satisfied, with no thought of saving the filter for reuse. At least, that's how I often end up using this facility.

Few of the other Photoshop books I checked out took the time to explain these characteristics of the Custom filter, and it's a shame. This is a virtual special effects playground that more users should be experimenting with.

# ■ Using Displacement Maps

The Displace filter deserves to be singled out as one of your easiest and most flexible filter customizing tools. It's related in some ways to the Texturizing filter we've already used, because it can apply additional files to govern how the filter works. However, instead of using the second image to texturize the original photo, Displace uses the color values in the additional file to determine how to move pixels around along a diagonal line. Moved how? I'll summarize the rules for you.

- If the displacement map has just one gray channel, the value of the pixel in the map at a particular position is used to move the image pixel in the same relative position. If the brightness of the pixel is 0 to 127, the pixel is moved southwesterly, with 0 representing the maximum amount of movement, and 127 the least. A value of 128 leaves the pixel in place. For values of 129 to 255, the pixel is moved in a northwesterly direction, with 255 representing the maximum amount of movement.

- If a displacement map has two or more channels (such as a grayscale image with a second, mask channel, or an RGB image), the first channel is used to determine the amount of horizontal movement, while the second channel is used to vary vertical movement. Additional channels are ignored.

- Since gray values are used, black-and-white bitmapped images can't be displacement maps.

Displacement maps are fun to play with because you can generate maps with fairly predictable results as well as maps that do things you never expected. For example, a map that consists of a smooth black-to-white grayscale gradient performs as you might expect. The portions of the map that are very dark will produce the most displacement in one direction, with the movement tapering off until the middle gray tones, and then reversing to the other direction for the lighter and lighter tones in the map. You can do all manner of twisting and warping in this mode. On the other hand, a map that consists of a texture or random lines that you create will do some rather weird things to an image. You'll want to experiment with displacement maps. You'll find some included with Photoshop; many more are available on-line.

## ■ Working with Displacement

To use the Displace filter, just follow these steps:

- Select Filter | Distort | Displace. The dialog box shown in Figure 10-10 will pop up.

- Choose the amount of displacement you want in both horizontal and vertical directions by typing values into the Horizontal Scale and Vertical Scale boxes. For example, if you specify 100 for both, grayscale values of 0 and 255 will produce movement of 128 pixels, and a value of 128 will generate the least movement. Lower scales will create proportionately less movement.

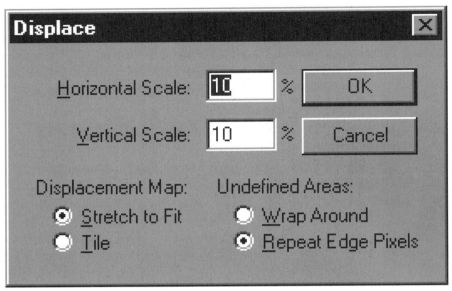

**Figure 10-10.** Displace Filter dialog box

- If the displacement map is not the same size as the selection, as will probably be the case unless you created the displacement map expressly for this image, you must decide whether Photoshop should stretch the map to fit the selection, or tile the map enough times to fill the selection.
- You should choose whether the filter should either fill in undefined areas by wrapping around to take pixels from the opposite edge, or simply repeat the pixels at the edge.
- Click on OK; then select the displacement map from your hard disk. Taking the image shown at left in Figure 10-11, I applied the Mezzotint and Streak maps supplied with Photoshop to the center and right portions, respectively. The maps used to produce the effects are shown in Figure 10-12.

# ■ Achieving Predictable Results

While almost any texture or random jottings you may insert in a map will generate some sort of displacement effect, you may want to create some predictable effects from time to time. The following exercise will help you visualize how the Displace filter works.

For my displaceable object, I used the 3D brick shown in Figure 10-13. You can probably figure out how I created it, using a texture filter, and then lightening and darkening various edges to give the 3D look.

**Figure 10-11.** Normal, Mezzotint, and Streak maps

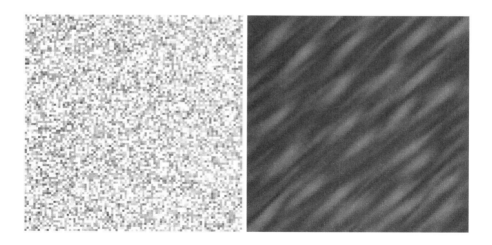

**Figure 10-12.** Mezzotint and Streak displacement maps

**Figure 10-13.** Brick test image

You won't have to go through all that, as I've included the image among the working files in the Chapter 10 folder on the CD-ROM.

Next, I created a pair of grayscale displacement maps. One, which starts out black in the middle, has a gradient that progresses to white at top and bottom. The other map is simply the first map inverted, using Image | Map | Invert. The two displacement maps are shown in Figure 10-14; the results of applying the top one to the brick appear in Figure 10-15.

Again, both maps are provided on the CD-ROM in the working files for this chapter. First, I applied the Grad01 map to the brick, using horizontal and vertical scales of 10 for each. The results are shown in Figure 10-15.

You can easily see that the dark, center portion of the gradient caused displacement quite different from the movement produced by the lighter top and bottom edges of the map. Using the reversed gradient on a new version of the brick, I got displacement of the exact opposite type, as shown in Figure 10-16.

What happens when you alter the scales? For Figure 10-17, I used settings of 15 for both horizontal and vertical scale. And, as the image stretches past the limits of the window at right, it wraps around to the left side, since I'd checked the "wrap" radio button.

**Figure 10-14.** Two gradients

**Figure 10-15.** Top gradient applied to brick with horizontal and vertical scales of 10

**Figure 10-16.**  Grad02 applied to the brick

**Figure 10-17.**  Grad01 applied with horizontal and vertical scales of 15

Look at Figure 10-18, in which I reduced the horizontal scale to 1 and bumped up the vertical scale to 15. The upper part of the image is stretched more than the lower part, which is actually squeezed together.

Finally, for Figure 10-19, I used a horizontal setting of 0 and a vertical setting of 100 to really stretch things, as you can see. It's often a good idea to experiment like this under tightly controlled conditions so you can see the effects of a filter, so that you'll be able to achieve more predictable results in your own work.

**Figure 10-18.** Grad01 map applied with horizontal scale 1 and vertical scale 15

**Figure 10-19.** Grad01 map applied with horizontal 0 and vertical scale 100

# ■ Moving On

Now that you know how to use custom filters, settings, and displacement maps, go ahead and experiment on your own. As you learned in this chapter, you don't need to know any programming to get some interesting results.  In the next chapter, we'll look at how to use some painting plug-ins to achieve artistic effects.

chapter

# 11

# Painting Plug-Ins

I'm not an artist. I just play one on Web TV. Using a variety of painting plug-ins within Photoshop and other image editors, I can produce results that look like they were rendered with brush, paints, and other traditional artists' tools. You can, too.

Because artistic filters simply push pixels around or change their colors, a huge number of them exist. There are even filters that generate effects that mimic the styles of specific artists. However, while digital effects can help process pixels in useful ways, no computer gadget can give you an artist's vision and imagination. In this chapter, we'll look at Photoshop's built-in filters as well as third-party filters that also provide painterly effects, such as Xaos Tools' Paint Alchemy. I'm going to use several different images as subject matter and apply several plug-ins to each so you can compare their effects.

## ■ In This Chapter:

- Uses for Painting Plug-ins
- Photoshop's Native Painting Filters
- Pencils and Other Media
- 3D Artistic Effects
- Other Effects
- Real Media Painting

# ■ Uses for Painting Plug-Ins

Painting filters have several uses you might not have thought of:

- Brush strokes or other effects can mask defects in an original photo. Dust, scratches, unwanted details, and other picture information that detracts from the look you want can be hidden with the right artistic plug-in. These kinds of filters all have one thing in common: They reduce the amount of information in an image by combining or moving pixels. Some overlay an image with a texture or pattern, while other plug-ins group similar colors together or transform groups of hues into new tones. The result is an image that has been softened, broken up, selectively increased in contrast, or otherwise "pixelated."

- Painting plug-ins can turn a photograph into a more abstract work of art. Instead of the harsh reality of the original image, we have a softer, more organic picture that appears to have been created, rather than captured.

- These plug-ins can help unify a Web thematically. You may have a collection of photographic images taken at different times and places under varying lighting. Application of a painting filter can give the images a semblance of unity as if all were created by, at the least, the same artist. That helps to tie graphic loose ends together and give your Web site a consistent look. Figure 11-1 shows two photos taken under very different lighting conditions, and then given a similar look with Photoshop's Spatter filter.

# ■ Photoshop's Native Painting Filters

We'll look at Photoshop's built-in artistic plug-ins first, so you can get an idea of the broad range of effects you can achieve without even purchasing a third-party add-on.

## Brush Strokes

Photoshop has quite a few filters that create the look of an artist's brushwork. But, as you work with the images in this chapter remember that: a great plug-in is no substitute for planning and executing your image carefully. Don't expect to find any sense in how Adobe has arranged these filters in its menus. Some brush effects are found in the Artistic submenu rather than under Brush Strokes, while Sketch includes the nonsketchy Chrome effect.

**Figure 11-1.** Original photos (left), processed with Spatter filter (right)

## Dry Brush

The Dry Brush filter is one of my favorites, because it mimics a natural-media effect—stroking with a brush that's almost devoid of paint—in a fairly predictable way. If I want to change a photograph into a painting, this is the filter I try first. It doesn't obscure as much detail as the typical watercolor, stipple, or impressionistic filter found in most image editing applications, but still has a distinct painted look.

Dry Brush posterizes your image, but produces more distinct banding than Dry Strokes. The bands of colors themselves become the strokes, as all similar colors in a particular area are reduced to one average hue. You can adjust the size of the brush—larger brushes apply broader strokes. The brush detail control allows you to change the amount of detail in each area by modifying the roughness of the edges. The texture control applies light, medium, or heavy texture to the image, using a series of three radio buttons. You can see how the Dry Brush filter works in the example in Figure 11-2. Increasing the brush size produces a more diffused look. Reducing brush detail to 1 and adding the maximum amount of texture makes the posterization effect more pronounced.

## Dark Strokes

The Dark Strokes filter has two effects on your image. It reduces the number of different tones in the image through a posterization-like effect that combines similar tones in an unusual way. Instead of grouping similar colors together, Dark Strokes makes dark tones darker and light tones lighter, increasing contrast. At the same time, each tone is rendered using diagonal brush strokes—short strokes for dark tones and longer strokes for light tones. You can see the effects quite clearly in the examples following.

While the default settings yield some interesting effects, I like to set the white intensity fairly high and reduce black intensity to cut back on the somber mood this filter can sometimes produce. It's a great filter for masking imperfect details that detract from, rather than enhance, a photo's appearance, as you can see at right in Figure 11-2.

## Fresco

Fresco is a technique in which water colors are applied to wet plaster (*fresco* is Italian for *fresh*) and allowed to dry, forming a permanent image on the wall or other structure containing the plaster. If you're an artist-type and can work fast, fresco is a great way to produce murals. Because the plaster is sticky and dries quickly, fresco images are distinguished by their short, jabby strokes. Like Dry Brush, Fresco adds a posterization effect to your image, but lightens the highlights more for a smeared look.

**Figure 11-2.** Unprocessed photo (left), Dry Brush (center), and Dark Strokes

## Spatter

The Spatter filter is another easy-to-use painterly effect that reproduces a look that would be generated if an airbrush could spatter out different color hues. While you can use the effect to soften portrait or landscape subjects, it also makes a great tool for creating endless abstract backgrounds. The Spray Radius slider adjusts the number of pixels covered by the sputtering spray emitted by your imaginary airbrush. The Smoothness control modifies the evenness of the effect. This filter makes great background textures for your Web pages. Figure 11-3 shows both the Fresco and Spatter effects.

## Watercolor

Watercolors produce their distinctive pastel effect because the pigments that dissolve in water are typically not as strong or opaque as those that can be carried in oil or acrylic paints. In addition, watercolors tend to soak into the paper, carrying bits of color outside the original strokes as the water spreads. The Watercolor filter offers the same soft, diffused effect with a bit more control for the electronic artist. It's a good plug-in for landscapes, female portrait subjects, or any image which can be improved with a soft look. You can specify the amount of brush detail, but will find that the blending effect of this filter doesn't work well with small, detailed strokes. Use higher values to get broad strokes

**Figure 11-3.** Fresco and Spatter

that show off the pastels and blended colors. At the same time, you'll often want to use low shadow intensity settings to avoid an overly contrasty look. Any of three levels of texture can also be applied.

## Angled Strokes

Angled Strokes must be used with care, since it produces such strong effects. This filter paints your image using diagonal strokes in one direction for the dark tones, and diagonal strokes going in the other direction to represent the light tones in an image. The Direction Balance is a key control. Slide it to the right to shift the emphasis toward the right-angled strokes; move to the left to emphasize the left-angled strokes. If you want to watch this control at work in its most dramatic mode, change the Stroke Length slider to the maximum (50) and the Sharpness control to 10. Your entire image will be rendered in left and right strokes that you can see clearly. Adjust Direction Balance to see the different effects you can achieve. With high resolution files, the effects may not be as noticeable unless you either reduce the size of the image to 25 to 50 percent of its original size before applying the filter (scale it back up when you're finished), or use a high sharpness setting. This filter can be applied to primary subjects, but also makes a good tool for creating artsy background textures for Web pages. In Figure 11-4, I used the Fade control to cut back on the amount of angled strokes applied to the image.

## Palette Knife

Take the knife that artists use to apply paints to their palette, and paint with it instead—you'll end up with a highly abstract image composed of irregular globs of pigment. That's the effect you get with the Palette Knife filter. The Stroke Size slider adjusts the size of the "knife" you're using, while the Stroke Detail control can be used to specify how much of the detail in your original image is retained. The Softness control increases or decreases the roughness of the edges of the palette strokes.

Although you can use this filter alone, it works well with other plugins, either as a first step to reduce the amount of detail before you apply a second filter, such as Watercolor or Grain. Textures, particularly canvas, can add to the painterly effect of this filter.

## Pointillize

This is one filter that will enrage artists and please everyone else. It purports to create a pointillistic image but don't expect to generate anything that reminds you of Georges Seurat. What you end up with is more of a randomized image with lots of little dots on it (many in colors

**Figure 11-4.** Original image (top), Watercolor (center), and Angled Strokes (bottom)

that you may not remember seeing in our original). Generally the pixelation represents the detail in your original photograph. You can select a cell size from 3 to 300 pixels. The most difficult thing about using this filter is selecting a compatible background color. All the spaces between dots are filled in with your current background color. If you're using the defaults, that's white. Softer pastels that match the predominate tones of your image make a better choice, unless you want the image to look as if it were overlaid with a snowstorm. Figure 11-5 shows how both the Palette Knife and Pointillize filters work.

## Wind

Both Photoshop's Wind filter and Kai's Power Tools' Pixelweather filters can create some amazing wind-blown and streaky effects. It can simulate dripping paint, or create an image reminiscent of a speedy superhero streaking by on his way to a crime scene. Choose your images carefully. When you have a picture with an empty or dark area that the wind effect can smear your image into, the results are much more impressive. You're not limited to left and right wind directions. I've gotten

**Figure 11-5.**  Palette Knife (top) and Pointillize (bottom) filters

some great effects by rotating an image, applying Wind or Pixel-weather, then rotating it back to its original orientation.

## Sprayed Strokes

This filter uses angled, sprayed strokes of wet paint. You can adjust the stroke length, direction, and radius of the spray emitted. This is a good filter to use for creating painterly images artsy backgrounds, or for adding a painted effect to pictures that have been processed with other filters. Figure 11-6 shows effects with Wind and Sprayed Strokes on a stained glass window in Spain. Check out the color version on the CD-ROM to appreciate the full effect.

## Underpainting

The Underpainting filter produces the effect you might get if you texturized an image in one layer, then combined it with an unaltered version of the same image in a layer applied on top of the first. It's otherwise similar to the Texturizer filter, but with the addition of Brush Size and Texture Coverage controls

## Paint Daubs

Yes, another brush strokes filter! Paint Daubs offers you six different brush types, a selection of brush sizes, and some sharpness controls. You can choose from simple, light rough, dark rough, wide sharp, wide blurry, or sparkle brush types.

**Figure 11-6.**  Wind and Sprayed Strokes

## Sponge

Real artists are so cocky they can paint with anything—even sponges. The effect is highly textured, with contrasting splotches of color. Those of us who need a little help with such a sloppy tool will like this Sponge filter, which creates images a dab at a time, using some controls that should be fairly familiar to you by this time. You can adjust brush size, definition, and smoothness using these sliders. Figure 11-7 shows the Underpainting, Paint Daubs, and Sponge effects.

## Sumi-e

Take a wet brush, load it with ink, and draw on a highly absorbent rice paper and what do you get? "Ink painting," or, in Japanese, sumi-e. This filter doesn't convert your image to monochrome, however, but it does add the effect of painting on blotter paper with ink. The controls are simple to master—just stroke width, stroke pressure, and contrast. This filter works best with landscapes or abstract images, because it tends to blur portrait subjects into unrecognizability.

## Water Paper

Water-based paints applied to wet paper will tend to migrate along the fibers, producing a blurry effect. The Water Paper filter lets you control

**Figure 11-7.** Underpainting (left), Paint Daubs (center), and Sponge (right)

over the length of the fibers, the brightness, and the relative contrast of the image. The effects you can get with this filter vary considerably as you manipulate the controls. The original image is shown at top in Figure 11-8, and the Sumi-e and Water Paper versions lower left and right respectively.

# ■ Pencils and Other Media

Of course, artists don't always work with paint. Pencils and other media are often used to create sketches that form the foundation for a later painting, or as an art end-product in themselves. Photoshop and other image editors offer a variety of plug-ins in this category. We'll look at a few of Photoshop's best in this section.

## Colored Pencil

Colored Pencil redraws your image, using the image's own colors, in a pencil-like effect. The strokes are applied in a cross-hatch fashion to delineate the edges of your image, while the current background color is allowed to show through the less detailed portions of your image, as if it were the paper on which the drawing was made. You have three controls. The Pencil Width slider adjusts the broadness of the strokes, while Stroke Pressure modifies their intensity. Paper Brightness determines how strongly the background color shows through smooth details in your image. This is a tricky filter to use, but I've found that using

**Figure 11-8.** Original image (top), Sumi-e (lower left), and Water Paper (lower right)

the brightness/contrast controls to increase contrast once the filter has been applied can approve the appearance dramatically.

## Graphic Pen

The Graphic Pen filter obliterates the detail in your image with a series of monochrome strokes that can be applied in right or left diagonal directions as well as horizontally and vertically. It is tricky to use, because it's easy to obscure all the detail in an image with overly enthusiastic stroking, lengthy strokes, or an unfortunate selection of light and dark balance. Many users often overlook the fact that Graphic Pen applies its strokes in the foreground color, leaving the background color behind to fill in the rest of the image area. Therefore, only the details in an image actually stroked by the pen remain.

If you use the default black/white foreground/background colors, you'll get a positive black and white image. Reverse the two (white foreground, black background) and you'll end up with a negative image. Some interesting effects can be produced by selecting complementary colors as foreground and background. The Stroke Length slider controls how much detail is preserved. If you don't like the right diagonal strokes applied as the default (they are a good compromise with images that have an equal mixture of horizontal and vertical components), you can change to vertical or horizontal strokes, as shown at lower left and lower right, respectively. Vertical strokes break up and show predominant horizontal lines well (say, a landscape), while horizontal strokes do the same thing for images with strong vertical strokes (such as a stand of pine trees.)

## Smudge Stick

This is a tough filter to like, because most of the effects Distort the image. But it does have at least one spectacular setting that I've come to use a lot. The basic filter paints your image in strokes that blend dark areas into the lighter areas. Figure 11-9, a photo of a statue at Notre Dame Cathedral in Paris, shows the Smudge Stick filter applied with the Highlight Area slider moved up to the maximum value of 20. This is my favorite use of the Smudge Stick filter, and not one you'd expect to get from casual experimentation.

## Rough Pastels

This filter transforms your image into a rough chalk drawing, using the default canvas texture as a background, or an alternate texture (such as brick, burlap, or sandstone) or your own file. The least amount of texture is applied to the brightest areas, while darker areas take on more of the underlying texture. You can picture how this filter works by imagining a canvas with chalk applied: the thicker the chalk, the less of the canvas texture shows through. You can specify stroke length, and

**Figure 11-9.** Clockwise from top left: original image, Colored Pencil, Smudge Stick, Graphic Pen

the amount of detail, and a specific texture to be used. You may find this filter modifies your image too strongly, and prefer to fade it.

## Conté Crayon

Georges Seurat is reputed to have developed the soft, smudgy, atmospheric effects that made Conté Crayon popular in the 19th Century. This version gives you deeply rendered dark tones, textured midtones, and clean whites. These crayons are commonly available in different colors, from black to sepia, and you can use the foreground and background colors of your application to control the hues to simulate actual commercial crayons. The original colors of your image are lost. The Foreground and Background Level controls can be used to adjust the amount of the foreground and background colors, respectively, used in the image. You may have to fiddle with these to find the right combination to represent your image without overpowering it. In addition, you can apply a texture using the standard controls already discussed for the Texturizer filter.

## Crosshatch

Crosshatch adds a cross pattern of pencil-like strokes to your image, adding texture without destroying all the original colors and detail of the original. It's a good arty effect with an unusual degree of control. Not only can you specify the stroke length and sharpness, but also the number of times in succession the filter is applied. The more repetitions, the stronger the effect. Figure 11-10 shows Rough Pastels, Conté Crayon, and Crosshatch effects.

## Ink Outlines

Adobe calls Ink Outlines a "corroded" ink drawing. It produces an image with the outlines and edges enhanced, but without losing the original colors. You can use it to create a cartoon-like appearance, or combine with other filters to generate a more painterly effect. You can adjust the length of the strokes, dark intensity, and light intensity. Moving the Light Intensity control all the way to the right can produce an especially interesting effect, as you can see in Figure 11-11 below.

# ■ 3D Artistic Effects

## Texturizer

The Texturizer filter should be one of your basic tools for applying textures to images or selections—but by no means should you make it your *only* surface-modifying tool. Most of what you can do with Texturizer you can also accomplish by loading a texture into a separate layer, but

**Figure 11-10.**  From top, Rough Pastels, Conté Crayon, Crosshatch

**Figure 11-11.**  Ink Outlines set at maximum Light Intensity

this filter is fast and highly automated, and already includes basic textures that will satisfy most of your needs. With Texturizer, you can select from the type of texture to be applied, using a drop down list. Brick, burlap, canvas, and sandstone are supplied, and these are suitable for a remarkable number of different images. However, you can also work with your own file. Custom textures can be created by scanning common household objects and surfaces. Don't worry too much about the size of the custom texture: if the image is too small to texturize your entire selection, it will be automatically tiled. Don't try to get away with a texture file that's too small, however: tiny images tiled can add a repeating pattern to your image that you probably won't like.

Textures are applied more strongly in those areas of your image where the brightness changes, so the results are not identical to what you'd get if you merged your image with another layer containing the texture. You can choose a light position for the imaginary light source used to produce the 3D texture's raised effect. Select a position at right angles to the "grain" of your texture, rather than parallel to it, in order to accentuate the 3D look. The scaling control specifies how large the texture is compared to the original image, and you can also set the amount of relief—the degree the texture is raised from the surface of the image. The texture can be inverted if you like. Figure 11-12 shows three different texture variations.

## Plaster

I'm not sure that the Plaster filter really gives you a plaster look, but it certainly does produce an outrageous and useful 3D effect. In some cases, your images will take on a molten plastic look, while in others

**Figure 11-12.** Top: original image. Bottom, from left: Burlap, Canvas, Sandstone.

**Figure 11-13.**  From top: Original image, Plaster, Note Paper, Bas Relief

you'll see more of a sunken effect.  Dark areas of the image are raised, while light areas are flattened or sunk into depressions.  The foreground and background colors of the application are used to transform your image. You can work with three different controls which operate much like their counterparts in the Bas Relief filter.   The Image Balance filter is important, since you can use it to control how much of the important detail in your original image shows up.  You'll find that even small adjustments can make a dramatic difference.  Select a light position and smoothness value to fine-tune your image.

## Note Paper

This filter creates the look of embossed paper, but with a flatter image than you get with Emboss or Bas Relief.  It really does look as if the image were created out of paper.  There are three controls at your disposal: image balance, graininess, and relief. This plug-in changes your color or gray-scale image into a high-contrast black-and-white image (if you're using the default black/white colors) or into an image using another color pair. It's worthwhile to experiment with color combinations to get the best effect. The key to using Note Paper is the Image Balance slider. Very small changes with this control make dramatic modifications to how much of your image appears embossed. You can also increase the amount of grain in the image or adjust the degree of relief applied. When grain is set to zero, a useful carved-from-plastic look results. You can also take an image given the no-grain treatment and apply a texture of your choice using the Texturizer filter.

## Bas Relief

Bas Relief makes the image appear to have been carved from stone, a look you can enhance by applying a sandstone texture to the selection using the Texturizer filter. Another great effect can be applied using the texture option in the Lighting Effects filter. The colors in your image are lost, since the current foreground and background colors are used to create your carving. As a result, this is one filter that works just as well with grayscale images as it does with color. If you want to retain hues, use the Emboss filter, instead. You can adjust the amount of detail retained from your original image, the position of the apparent light source used to illuminate the resulting 3-D image, and the smoothness of the surface. When experimenting with this filter, don't forget the psychology of lighting: humans expect objects to be lit from above, and, usually from one side or the other. You'll get the most realistic raised effects if you position the light source at top, top left, or top right. Move the light underneath, and you'll get anything from a "horror" effect to a reversal of the 3D look—your image may appear to be depressed into the surface rather than raised above it.

## Craquelure

If you want an ancient example of how a bug becomes a feature, look no farther than the Craquelure filter. In only a few short hundred years, the bane of ancient artists has become a quality that professional photographers and, now, computer image workers, will actually pay for. Paints applied to canvas or some other surface don't retain their pristine surface, broken only by carefully-applied brush strokes, for very long. The paints themselves aren't stable, composed as they are of exotic substances that can include egg whites, clay, and weird chemicals or plants used as pigment. Nor can you count on the substrate to keep its shape and size forever. Something as simple as fluctuations in temperature can cause paintings to develop a network of cracks. Pro photographers sometimes have this texture applied to their photographs to give them an Old Masters patina. You can achieve a similar effect, which adds a nice 3D look, using the Craquelure filter.

You can control the crack spacing, depth, and brightness. The default spacing of 15 gives you a good mixture of cracks and image area. Decreasing the spacing much below 10 makes the cracks so wide that the raised, embossed portion of the image may be just a few isolated bumps. Increasing the spacing to 50 or more produces an image that resembles your original, with a sparse distribution of cracks. The depth and brightness settings change the appearance of the cracks themselves. You'll find that deeper or shallower cracks can dramatically change the effect. Check out Figure 11-14 for an example.

## ■ Other Effects

The following effects are difficult to pigeonhole into any category, but you'll find them useful for an impressive array of artsy looks.

### Cutout

The Cutout filter is an unusual posterizing technique in which the image shapes are seemingly built up from similarly-colored cutouts of paper. You can combine this filter with Emboss to make the shapes look as if they were actually cut out of paper. The Number of Levels control specifies the number of tones used to posterize the image. Edge Simplicity controls the complexity of the cutout shapes, while Edge Fidelity ad-

**Figure 11-14.**  Craquelure effect

justs how well the shapes match the actual outlines of the underlying image.

## Mosaic

True mosaic is an artistic process of creating pictures by inlaying small pieces of colored stone or glass in mortar. Photoshop has two Mosaic filters, which resulted from the merging of Adobe Gallery Effects (which had its own Mosaic) into Photoshop Version 3. The original Mosaic filter, found in the Pixelate menu, is useless unless you want to obscure some faces or license plates, as on cop reality shows. The Texture|Mosaic Tiles filter, on the other hand, creates irregularly-shaped 3D tiles from your image, and embeds them in grout. You can vary the size of the tiles, the width of the grout, and the relative darkness of the grout. This filter offers a more organic, human-made look with added control.

## Poster Edges

This filter transforms your image into a poster by converting full-color or gray-scale images into reduced color versions by combining similar colors into bands of a single hue. This is similar to the posterization effect, but goes a step further by outlining all the important edges in your image with black. In many cases, the finished photo looks as if it were an original drawing that was hand-colored in poster fashion.

Poster Edges gives you three controls, so you can adjust the relative thickness of the black lines used to outline the edges, and specify their darkness or intensity. A third slider lets you specify the degree of posterization—that is, how many tones are used to produce the effect. Note that with this filter the value represents only a relative degree, not the actual number of tones used (which is the case with the Photoshop native Posterization effect.) Figure 11-15 shows the Cutout, Mosaic Tiles, and Poster Edges effects.

**Figure 11-15.** Cutout, Mosaic Tiles, and Poster Edges

## Diffuse Glow

Diffuse Glow can produce a radiant luminescence in any image, which seems to suffuse from the subject and fill the picture with a wonderful luster. At the same time, this plug-in softens harsh details. It's great for romantic portraits, or for lending a fantasy air to landscapes. Diffuse Glow works equally well with color and black-and-white images. This is a particularly easy filter to use. Almost any combination of settings, including the defaults, look good. But to get the most from Diffuse Glow, you'll want to master its simple controls.

The Graininess slider adds or reduces the amount of grain applied to an image. A large amount obscures unwanted detail and adds to the dreamy look of the image. The Glow Amount control adjusts the strength of the glow, as if you were turning up the voltage on a light source. The higher the setting, the more glow spread throughout your picture. The Clear Amount slider controls the size of the area in the image that is not affected by the glow. You can use this control with the Glow Amount slider to simultaneously specify how strong a glow effect is produced, as well as how much of the image is illuminated by it. The current background color becomes the color of the glow. Figure 11-16 shows an image processed with this filter.

**Figure 11-16.**  Diffuse Glow

### Torn Edges

The Torn Edges filter gives your image (what else?) torn edges. It converts color images to two-color, using the current foreground and background hues. As with previous "picky" filters, the Image Balance control is the most important, as it governs how much of your original image will be viewable in the final version. You can also adjust smoothness and contrast, and may need to experiment to get the best settings, since even small adjustments in any of these three controls can produce dramatically different images.

### Facet Filter

This filter changes blocks of pixels that are similar in color to one tone, producing a faceted effect like the face of a diamond (or maybe like the face of Bizarro Superman, if you remember him.) This is a kind of posterization, but with the reduction in number of colors taking place in a seemingly randomized way over the entire image. Details are masked, so this is an excellent filter to use with grainy, dust-laden, or otherwise imperfect photographs. The Facet filter has no dialog box or options; you apply it directly to any selection or an entire image. The effect becomes more pronounced with repeated applications. Just use Ctrl/Command-F to apply the filter several times until you get the look you desire.

### Stamp

This filter re-creates the effects you get with rubber or wooden stamps. Artists and artisans have often produced interesting, repeatable patterns by carving an image out of a block of wood, or from a piece of rubber or linoleum glued to a block of wood. Since world supplies of linoleum dried up when all the linoleum mines in Macronesia were closed down, the electronic equivalent provided by the Stamp filter has been the closest we can get to the original effect. You can adjust light/dark balance, and should do so carefully to insure that the important outlines of your image are represented in your finished stamp. The Smoothness control can adjust how rough the stamp's outlines appear. This filter uses the foreground and background colors you've selected, transforming your photo into a two-tone, stencil-like image. Figure 11-17 shows the Torn Edges, Facet, and Stamp filters at work.

# ■ Real Media Painting

If you have just about any non-Photoshop image editor, such as PhotoImpact, Picture Publisher, Corel Photo-Paint or, especially, MetaCreations Painter, you have access to tools that allow you to paint using

**Figure 11-17.** Torn Edges, Facet, and Stamp filters

realistic paintbrushes, pencils, and other media. You can paint from scratch, or apply individual brush strokes to your images. If you use Photoshop, you'll need an add-on plug-in like Xaos Tools' Paint Alchemy. This next section will deal with Paint Alchemy, as it can be used with any Photoshop plug-in compatible image editor.

Paint Alchemy has been a mainstay plug-in in the Macintosh world for many years, and was ported over to Windows awhile ago. Corel thought enough of this filter toolset to bundle it with Corel Photo-Paint. Alchemy can apply an amazing number of brush strokes to your image,

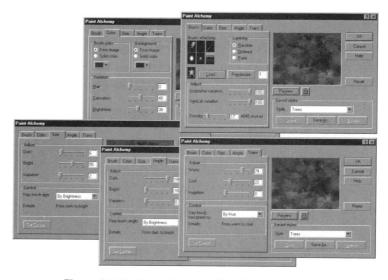

**Figure 11-18.** Paint Alchemy offers five control tabs.

using stored sets of brushes or those you define. A series of tabbed dialog boxes, shown in Figure 11-18, allow you to specify everything from brush shape, color, size, and angle to transparency.

Alchemy can produce realistic brush strokes or create abstract patterns with equal facility, as you can see in Figures 11-19 through 11-22. Figure 11-19 shows an unprocessed image, a woodsy scene with trees

**Figure 11-19.**  Unprocessed image

**Figure 11-20.**  Fine-etched brush treatment

and a free-flowing brook.  Figure 11-20 is the same image given a finely-etched brush treatment. For this graphic, I applied the filter to a duplicate layer of the original, then adjusted the opacity so that about 20 percent of the unprocessed image showed through.

Then, for Figure 11-21, I selected a splotchier brush to end up with an apparently random pattern useful as a Web page background.  You

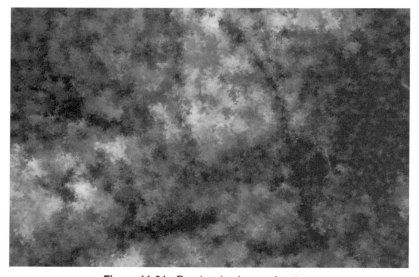

**Figure 11-21.**  Random background pattern

**Figure 11-22.**  Typical Web page using painting effects

can see how a background produced with Alchemy might be applied in Figure 11-22.

## ■ Moving On

We're going to wrap up the book with two chapters that showcase some of the other special effects you can achieve with plug-ins, including a few that we haven't used much.  Chapter 12 concentrates on the Extensis product line, which is included in fully functional trial versions on the CD-ROM bundled with this book.  Chapter 13 is a potpourri of many different effects.

# chapter
# 12

# Extensis Tools

After MetaCreations, Extensis is easily the most influential provider of plug-ins for Photoshop-compatible image editors. Extensis's offerings are available for both Windows and Mac platforms; Ulead, in contrast, at this writing has plug-ins only for Windows machines. Andromeda has a great selection of cross-platform tools, but many of them are more specialized than the modules available from Extensis.

Because I've gotten permission to include try-out versions of Extensis products on the CD-ROM bundled with this book, I'm going to devote a chapter to showing you what can be done with these versatile plug-ins. Although I have used the older version of Extensis products with Photoshop 5.0 with no problems, the company has posted free updates for registered users that are more compatible with the latest version.

## ■ In This Chapter

- PhotoTools
- Mask Pro

# ■ PhotoTools

PhotoTools has seven components. PhotoText enhances the text-handling capabilities of Photoshop in ways that will be especially useful for pre-Version 5 users of the program. PhotoBars make it possible to add button bars with frequently used commands available at the click of an icon in the bar.    PhotoTools' remaining PhotoEffects are PhotoCast-Shadow, PhotoButton, PhotoEmboss, PhotoGlow, and PhotoBevel. We'll look at each of them in this section.

## PhotoText

Like Photoshop 5.0's Type tool, PhotoText allows you to mix fonts, colors, sizes, and styles without being forced to start a new block of text for each change.  You also have the same control over leading, kerning, tracking, alignment, and scaling as in Photoshop 5. However, PhotoText has quite a few cool features you won't find in Adobe's latest upgrade, including the ability to define styles, plus a more useful preview window, as you can see in Figure 12-1.  The two dialog boxes differ slightly in Mac and Windows versions; the Windows version is shown.

**Figure 12-1.** PhotoText preview window

You'll notice that PhotoText looks like a mini-application in its own right. In the Windows version, as in any application, it has menus and buttons. The PhotoText menu allows you to start new text blocks within the preview window and to open or save text blocks to your disk, either in PhotoText format or as standard text files. Text blocks stored in the PhotoText format can be edited at any time until you choose to apply the layer.

The Edit menu supplies standard word processor commands for selecting, copying, cutting, pasting, and undoing text. The Font, Text, and Spacing menus duplicate the text formatting commands found in the toolbar. The Style menu allows defining and applying format settings, and the Window manual can be used for zooming in and out in the preview window if you'd rather not use the Zoom tool. Figure 12-2 shows the headings for the PhotoText menu bar.

The toolbars should also be fairly familiar to anyone who's used a word processing program. As you can see in Figure 12-3, a pull-down list of fonts is available, with buttons setting text as normal, bold, italic, underlined, shadow, strikeout, small caps, and all caps. To the right of these are buttons for specifying left and right flush, centered text, and full justification.

The lists to the right of these toolbars (shown in Figure 12-3) adjust font size, tracking and kerning (the space between selected characters), leading (the spacing between lines), and character width. Note that arrows to the left of each property (pointing to the left and right in Windows, and up and down on Macs) allow dialing in specific values, while the down-pointing arrows to the right enable choosing a value from a drop-down list.

**Figure 12-2.**   PhotoText menu bar

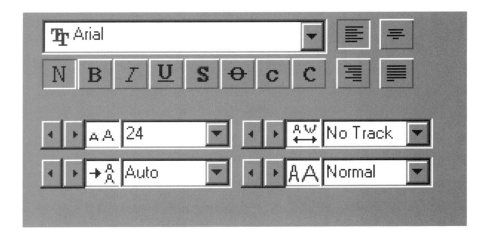

**Figure 12-3.** Toolbars

Additional controls are available at the left of the preview window. From the top in Figure 12-4, these include the Text tool (for entering and selecting text); the Move tool (for repositioning or resizing text blocks); the Zoom tool (click to zoom in, Alt/Option click to zoom out); the Hand tool (to move the image around in the preview window); the Eyedropper tool (to choose a color in the preview to apply to the text); and the Color display, showing foreground and background colors. (Click to select colors from the Color Picker.)

Below the toolbox are radio buttons that show whether Anti-aliasing is turned on or off, and an X/Y coordinates display that reveals the current position of the cursor.

If you often find you want to reuse a particular set of settings, you can save them as a Style by selecting Edit Styles menu. Give the Style a name, and save, as shown in Figure 12-5.

## PhotoBars

PhotoBars is a clever add-on that allows you to create your own toolbars with your favorite commands and menu selections, making them available with one click without the need to wade through a thicket of nested menu layers. PhotoTools creates by default three different PhotoBars, which you can hide or reveal individually. The default bars are shown in Figure 12-6.

**Figure 12-4.** Toolbox and other controls

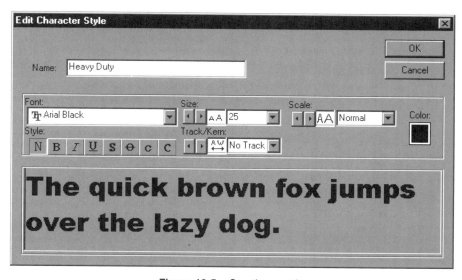

**Figure 12-5.** Creating a style

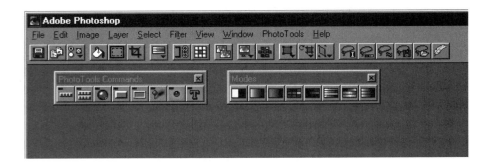

**Figure 12-6.** Default PhotoBars

One bar is deposited directly underneath Photoshop's menu. You'll find yourself saving dozens of clicks and keystrokes with these buttons alone. They provide one-click access to functions like stroking and cropping a selection, changing image or canvas size, inverting and saving selections, or duplicating an image. Do you have lots of Mode changes to do? All the common Mode commands are included on another button bar. Instead of wading through Image | Mode | Indexed Color, just click on the Indexed Color icon. PhotoTools' own functions are located on a third button bar, which can be used to edit or create button bars, or activate one of the PhotoEffects described shortly. For any of the bars, pass the mouse cursor over a button to learn its function.

Button bars can float above your image, as shown in Figure 12-6 or be embedded in the side of your image editor's window, as you can see in Figure 12-7. You may also create custom button bars. A bar I generated to provide click-access to a selection of plug-in filters is embedded at the left side of the screen. Macintosh users can also define their own button shapes or use Extensis's SmartBar, a floating palette that automates creating toolbars and buttons.

Windows users who want to create button icons will have to create the icons within an image editor capable of producing 16-color files measuring 19 pixels wide by 17 pixels tall. I did this in Photoshop, originally using an RGB image which I reduced to 16 colors with Image | Mode | Indexed Color, specifying Adaptive Palette and specifying 4

**Figure 12-7.** Embedded PhotoBars

bits per pixel as the color depth from the drop-down list. You can also choose Other as a color depth and type in 16 colors manually. The dialog box for customizing a new button is shown in Figure 12-8.

## PhotoEffects

The five PhotoEffects plug-ins are easy to use—we've already applied most of them in the previous chapters of this book. In this section, I'll provide some quick examples so you can review how they work. The descriptions will also help you decide if you want to purchase these Extensis products if you already don't have a copy, or haven't explored the try-out versions on the CD-ROM bundled with this book.

These filters all have some commands in common. All work with on-screen previews that provide a real-time glimpse of what your image will look like when the filter is applied, with all the layers active (not just the layer you are working with.) You can take advantage of multiple undo/redo to experiment, and then backtrack if you don't like the results. You can save settings for reuse or apply the presets Extensis provides with each filter.

**PhotoCastShadow:** This is a filter that allows creating drop shadows, cast shadows, and variations with completely control over where the shadow falls, how it blurs, and other factors. You can even create a "perspective blur" in which the shadow gets fuzzier the farther it falls from the original object—just as in real life. Figure 12-9 shows the dialog box, and Figure 12-10 shows the kind of effects you can get.

**PhotoButton:** This filter provides all the tools you need to create cool custom button shapes, working from standardized shapes like square, round, and polygon. You can edit the shapes, rotate them, and control radius and bevel geometry and other factors. There are two

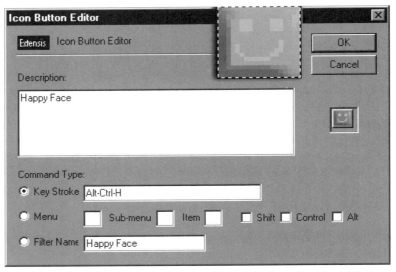

**Figure 12-8.** Custom button dialog box, shown with an enlarged version of the icon that will be pasted.

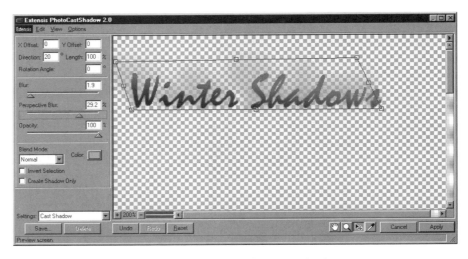

**Figure 12-9.** PhotoCastShadow dialog box

separate tabs to the dialog box: Shape, to control the shape, and size, as you can see in Figure 12-11; and Color, which is used to modify the color and surface texture of the bevel, illumination angle, and highlighting, as you can see in Figure 12-12.

**PhotoBevel:** This filter raises the edge of a selection, making it appear to have shadows on its inside and outside edges. You can control feathering, softness, highlights, shadow intensity, and light direction, and choose from flat, round, slope, or double bevels. This is a great tool

**Figure 12-10.** Shadow effect with PhotoCastShadow

**Figure 12-11.** PhotoButton Shape tab

**Figure 12-12.** PhotoButton Color tab

for creating specialized buttons. One cool touch is the way each of the possible effects appears instantly in the preview window as you scroll through the drop-down list of choices. Figure 12-13 shows the PhotoBevel dialog box.

**PhotoEmboss:** This filter is unlike any embossing filter you may have used. You have complete control over the type of embossing, and the contrast, highlights, shadows, and softness of the effect, in addition to the lighting direction. Figure 12-14 shows the PhotoEmboss dialog box.

**PhotoGlow:** You can create neon sign effects, soft luminescence, or bright gleams using the PhotoGlow filter. You have complete control over the stroke shape and width, how abruptly the glow diffuses around the edges, as well as the opacity, color, and blending mode. Figure 12-15 shows a typical effect.

# ■ PhotoFrame

PhotoFrame is a sensational plug-in that lets you apply a good-looking border effect or frame to an image, using your own frame files or any of the 150 available on the CD-ROM bundled with the filter. PhotoFrame is also compatible with frame files supplied with Auto F/X Photo/Graphic Edges. You'll find brush-stroke frames, and camera effects, or use natural media like charcoal. A different frame file can be

**Figure 12-13.**   PhotoBevel dialog box

**Figure 12-14.**   PhotoEmboss dialog box

**Figure 12-15.** PhotoGlow dialog box

used both for the edges and the frame's background, and you can apply up to three frames per image.

PhotoFrame works with any JPEG file as well as its own portfolio of frames, available in two CD-ROM volumes. Volume 1 includes painted edge effects, such as stucco, watercolor, canvas, and pebble board. Volume 2 adds digital effects, like orange peel, filmstrip and wave effects. Figure 12-16 shows the PhotoFrame dialog box.

# ■ Mask Pro

If you need to make complex selections to isolate pieces of art on your Web page, Mask Pro has the tools. Although it's intended as a professional-level accessory that aids graphics gurus in creating sophisticated composite images, Web designers can take advantage of its features, as well. It does a particularly good job with difficult edges, such as trees or hair.

Mask Pro puts color matching to work to create finely tuned masks. Use a green-tipped brush to define the colors that are "kept" or unmasked. A red-tipped brush can be applied to determine which colors are to be masked or dropped. You can also use magic brushes, magic wands, and other painting tools to mask areas. A Photoshop-like Pen tool can also be used to draw paths that become part of the mask. You may define the size of the brush, the softness of the edge, and the threshold and transition between masked and unmasked areas.

Although it's a plug-in, Mask Pro looks like a mini-application in operation, with a toolbox, several slider windows, and a navigation window, as you can see in Figure 12-17.

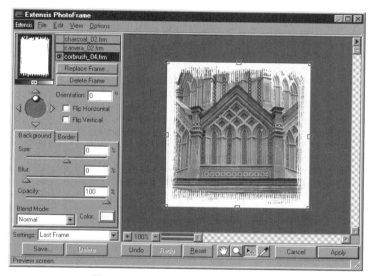

**Figure 12-16.** PhotoFrame dialog box

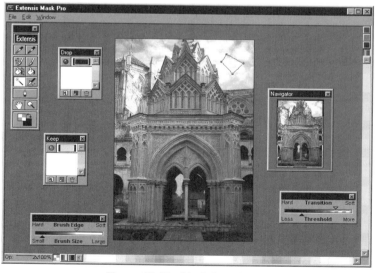

**Figure 12-17.** Mask Pro window

# ■ Moving On

In the final chapter of this book, we're going to bring together a host of different effects, using the broadest possible range of plug-ins, for one last Web graphics gallery. We'll revisit some old friends and see how some of the more specialized filters can be put to work.

**Color 48.** Add some bubbles to give a liquid look.

**Color 49.** Glass, shadow, gradient, plastic, and perspective techniques were combined to create this image.

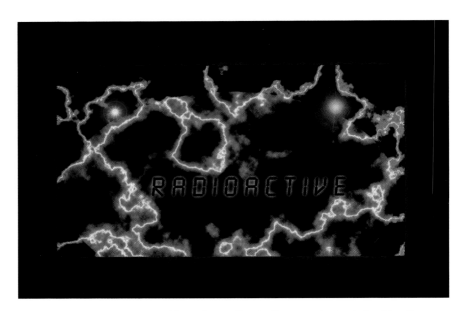

**Color 50.** Believe it or not, Photoshop's Clouds filter was the basis for this effect.

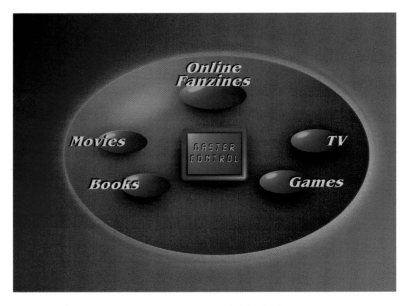

**Color 51.** 3D buttons make great fodder for image maps.

**Color 52.** The plaque from Chapter 2 was given yet another look with a stronger gradient.

**Color 53.** Photoshop's Plastic Wrap filter helped create this image.

**Color 54.** Looks like that fire is still out of control and, thanks to the Pinch filter, has warped the burning house.

**Color 55.** Photoshop's Dry Brush filter

**Color 56.** KPT's Video Feedback filter—applied to the photo shown in the inset—generated this eerie landscape.

**Color 57.** Poster Edges can turn an ordinary photo into a postcard.

**Color 58.** Ink Outlines, with some texture added

**Color 59.** The Find Edges filter is great for images with strong lines.

# chapter
# 13

# Effects Roundup

Although I've tried to provide you with scads of examples through-out this book, the need to explain how most of the effects were done sharply limited the number of cool samples I could provide in the text proper. The real showcases for the Web graphics I created with plug-ins are in three different locations: the CD-ROM bundled with this book, which contains every figure in glorious full color; the 32-page color insert, which I've used to display the very best of the images I developed for the book, and this chapter, which offers a monochrome review of some of the best filters and the effects you can create with them. While some of the images in this chapter are shown in color in the insert, I urge you to view the originals on the CD-ROM to appreciate the full depth of the effects.

The descriptions in this chapter will be brief and confined to the captions. By now you should have a good idea of how to use the plug-ins we've explored, and know that my experiments are only a jumping off point for your own. Have fun!

**Figure 13-1.** Andromeda makes a great set of filters that reproduce photographic effects. I applied the Screens filter, using the Chips African preset. Then I pasted a copy of the original image in a new layer and erased the effect around the musicians' faces.

**Figure 13-2.** Using the same original image, I applied Sharpen Edges twice, and then used Andromeda's Star filter to create this halo effect with beams of light.

**Figure 13-3.** Xaos Tools' Terrazzo filter creates kaleidoscopic effects based on any portion of an image that you choose. The results make great abstract patterns for backgrounds or can be used to add life and movement to a static image.

**Figure 13-4.** The Psychedelic filter found in Corel Photo-Paint produces this effect.

**Figure 13-5.** Solarization is a photographic effect in which the partially developed film is exposed to light, reversing some of the tones.  The digital effect is better because it can be carefully controlled.

**Figure 13-6.** This amazingly realistic effect was produced by selecting different portions of the house, and then applying Eye Candy's fire filter.

**Figure 13-7.** The fire was extinguished by a careful application of the Corel Photo-Paint Vasili (Kandinski) filter. This is a great abstract effect for backgrounds or Web art.

**Figure 13-8.** Corel Photo-Paint has a good collection of filters that are quite different from those you'll find in Photoshop. This Vortex Brushed filter is an example.

**Figure 13-9.** The Corel Vortex Mosaic gives some of the loveliest painting effects we've found, as you can see in this example.

**Figure 13-10.** Don't be afraid to experiment with plug-ins. I faded in a copy of the original image to reduce the effect of Corel's Wave Pager filter.

**Figure 13-11.** Corel's Water Marker filter produces a unique effect, unlike anything you'll find in other filter sets.

**Figure 13-12.** Variations can look better than the original. I applied Eye Candy's Antimatter filter to the image shown in Figure 13-7 to get this look.

**Figure 13-13.** Figures 13-13 through 13-16 offer ways to disguise an ugly CEO. First, try using an old-timey halftone effect to make it look like the photo was goofed up at the printer.

**Figure 13-14.** Mask all those defects by applying a painting filter, in this case Photoshop's Angled Strokes.

**Figure 13-15.** Here, Kai's Power Tools' Planar Tiling filter adds a 3D look to the image.

**Figure 13-16.** If all else fails, you can resort to the police reality show ploy, and render the boss anonymous through the use of the Mosaic filter.

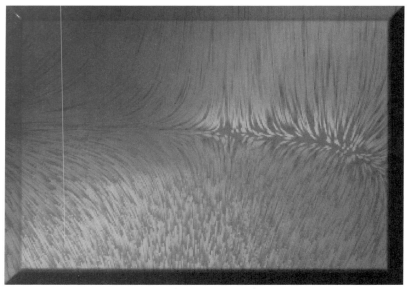

**Figure 13-17.** This button effect was created by applying Eye Candy's Fur filter to a gradient, and then adding an Inner Bevel.

**Figure 13-18.** A clutch of special effects were applied to this image: Eye Candy's Jiggle filter, Water Drops, and Outer Bevel, all applied to a rainbow gradient.

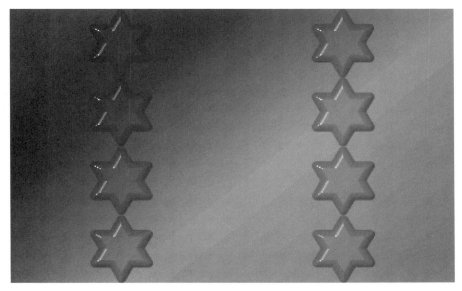

**Figure 13-19.** Extensis's PhotoButton plug-in can create up to 64 copies of a button at once. You can use this feature to create variations to give a Web page different looks based on the same theme.

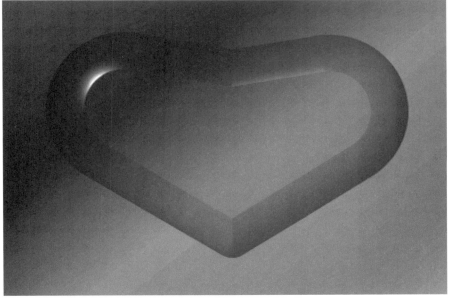

**Figure 13-20.** You can alter the shape of the selection used with Extensis's PhotoButton plug-in.

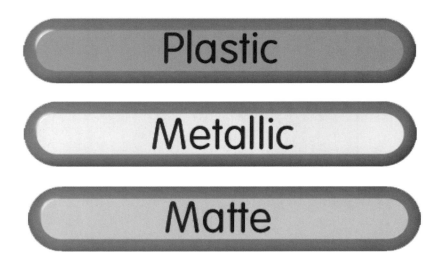

**Figure 13-21.** Some subtle differences in surface texture give buttons their own look. The buttons above have plastic, metallic, and matte sheens applied by Extensis PhotoButton.

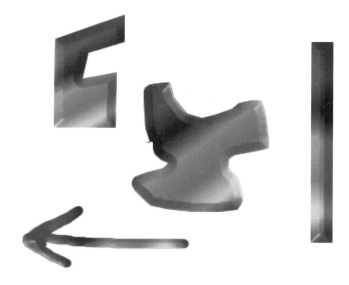

**Figure 13-22.** Buttons don't have to be oval or elliptical! These shapes were all transformed into whimsical buttons using Ulead's any-shape buttonizer.

**Figure 13-23.** Extensis's PhotoBevel plug-in can turn any shape into a button.  Here, I applied a copper gradient to a circular selection and applied a double bevel with a high degree of softness specified for the bevel edges.

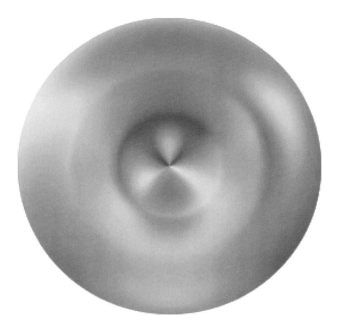

**Figure 13-24.** Sometimes you just have to play around and see what happens.  I never imagined that applying KPT's Vortex Tiling plug-in to the button in FIgure 13-23 would produce this result until I tried it.

**Figure 13-25.** KPT's Spheroid Designer added the texture to this button, and the Glass Lens filter gave it some sheen and shadow. I added a PhotoBevel to complete the effect.

## Text Effects
## Text Effects

**Figure 13-26.** These two effects were produced using Eye Candy's Cutout and Inner Bevel filters, both applied to text filled with a Copper gradient.

**Figure 13-27.** For the text at top, I took Figure 13-26's same text with a Copper gradient and applied Eye Candy's Glass filter. The text at bottom was roughed up with some monochrome Noise, and then beveled with Eye Candy's Outer Bevel filter.

**Figure 13-28.** Some sophisticated effects are easy to achieve. For this jaunty text, I used a soft-edged brush to paint the letters in black. Then I selected the text in one letter, using Select | Similar to expand the selection to the other letters. Then, I used Select | Grow and applied a rainbow gradient. Eye Candy's Inner Bevel finished off the effect. Because not all the original text was selected, it remains as a black drop-shadow with no extra work required!

**Figure 13-29.** KPT's Video Feedback filter creates some great looking backgrounds, like this one applied to a rainbow gradient.

**Figure 13-30.** Bevel applied to the gradient before applying the Video Feedback filter.

# Glossary

**Active Desktop:** Microsoft's term for the interface built into Windows 98 and Microsoft Internet Explorer 4.0 and later, in which the browser and user's desktop are merged into one working area.

**additive colors:** The red, green, and blue (RGB) colors used to display images on a monitor (and therefore by browsers); all three colors added together produce white. Web graphics are usually prepared in an image editor's RGB mode.

**adjustment layer:** A Photoshop 4 and 5 feature that can be used to modify the contrast, brightness, color, and other parameters of the layers below it without changing the pixels themselves. Adjustment layers can be edited, turned on and off, and otherwise manipulated to provide effects to the layers they are applied to.

**airbrush:** Originally an artist's tool that sprays a fine mist of paint to create soft-edged effects. The digital version in most image editors includes user-configurable brushes that can apply a spray of a selected tone at adjustable "pressure" levels to an area.

**alpha channel:** A grayscale layer of an image used to store selections.

**animated GIF:** A GIF file that contains the multiple images of an animation; these images are displayed one after another by a Web browser to produce the illusion of movement.

**animation:** Computer graphics used to prepare moving sequences of images. On the WWW, you'll find animations in the form of animated GIFs, QuickTime Movies, and other formats.

**anti-aliasing:** A process that minimizes jaggy diagonal lines by using in-between tones to smooth the appearance of the line. Anti-aliasing helps produce smoother images for Web graphics, even at relatively low resolutions.

**applet:** A small application, especially one produced for Web use with the Java language supported by the latest browsers.

**applications program interface (API):** A shared intermediate interface that allows a broad range of hardware and software products to communicate. Plug-ins use APIs to integrate filters with image editors or to link a program to scanners and digital cameras.

**ascender:** The portion of a lowercase letter that rises above the top of the main portion of the letter.

**aspect ratio:** The proportions of an image—e.g., 1024 x 768-, 800 x 600, and 640 x 480-pixel Web pages all have the same 4:3 aspect ratio or proportions.

**attribute:** Characteristics of an object, including color, font, or line width.

**background:** The color or pattern of a Web page on which text and images are displayed. Also, the bottom layer of a Photoshop image.

**backlighting:** Lighting effect produced when the main light is located behind the subject.

**bandwidth:** The amount of information that a communications link can carry at one time.

**baseline:** An imaginary line on which type rests.

**Bézier curve:** An editable curved line.

**bilevel:** An image that stores only black-and-white information, with no gray tones; Photoshop calls such images bitmaps.

**bit map:** A description of an image that represents each pixel as a number in a row and column format.

**black:** The color formed by the absence of reflected or transmitted light– e.g., the combination of 100 percent values of cyan, magenta, and yellow ink (in the subtractive color system) or 0 values of red, green, and blue light (in the additive color system).

**blur:** To reduce the contrast between pixels that form edges in an image, softening it.

**brightness:** The amount of light and dark shades in an image. The relative lightness or darkness of the color, usually measured as a percentage from 0% (black) to 100% (white).

**browser:** An application like Netscape Navigator or Microsoft Internet Explorer that lets users access World Wide Web servers and view HTML pages and other content.

**burn:** To darken part of an image.

**cache:** An area of memory used to store information, such as a Web page and its graphics, so it can be accessed more quickly than data placed in slower RAM, on a hard disk, or in other storage.

**calibration:** Adjusting a device such as a scanner, monitor, or printer so its output represents a known standard.

**cast:** A tinge of color in an image, usually an undesired color.

**channel:** One of the layers that make up an image, such as the red, green, and blue channels of an RGB image, or the cyan, magenta, yellow, and black channels of a CMYK image. Alpha channels are additional layers used to represent masks or selections.

**clickable image:** A graphic or image map in an HTML document that can be clicked on to retrieve associated URLs and their contents.

**client-side image map:** A clickable image map that includes the URLs available for access, and their coordinates on a page, directly on the page itself, so a Web browser supporting this feature can follow the designated hyperlinks without intervention by the server.

**clip art:** Artwork available for scanning, desktop or Web publishing, and other uses with few restrictions.

**clone:** To copy pixels from one part of an image to another, as with Photoshop's rubber stamp tool.

**CMYK color model:** A model that defines all possible colors in percentages of cyan, magenta, yellow, and black.

**color correction:** To change the balance of colors in an image, most often to improve the accuracy of the rendition or to compensate for deficiencies in the color separation and printing process.

**color depth:** The number of bits of information used to represent color values in an image; the higher the number of bits, the greater the number of colors (and shades) that can be represented.

**complementary color:** Generally, the opposite hue of a color on a color wheel, which is called the direct complement. For example, green is the direct complement of magenta.

**compression:** Reducing the size of a file by encoding using smaller sets of numbers that don't include redundant information. Some kinds of compression, such as JPEG, can degrade images, while others, including GIF and PNG, preserve all the detail in the original.

**continuous tone:** Describes images that contain tones from the darkest to lightest with an infinite range of variations in between.

**contrast:** The range of individual tones between the lightest and darkest shades in an image.

**convolve:** A process used by imaging filters that incorporates the values of surrounding pixels in calculating new values for sharpening, blurring, or other effects.

**crop:** To trim an image or page by adjusting the boundaries.

**darken:** The process of selectively changing pixel values to darker ones.

**default:** The value or parameter used for a plug-in, tool, action, or function unless you specify otherwise using a dialog box or some other method.

**defloat:** To merge a floating selection with the underlying image.

**defringe:** To remove the outer edge pixels of a selection, often when merging a selection with an underlying image.

**desaturate:** To reduce the purity or vividness of a color, as with Photoshop's Sponge tool. Desaturated colors appear washed out and diluted.

**descender:** The portion of a lowercase letter that extends below the baseline, such as the tail on the letter y.

**diffusion:** The random distribution of tones in an area of an image, often used to represent a larger number of tones.

**displacement map:** A Photoshop file used by the Displace filter to control the shifting of pixels in an image horizontally or vertically to produce a particular special effect.

**dithering:** A method of simulating tones that can't be represented at the current color depth by grouping the dots into clusters of varying size. The mind merges these clusters and the surrounding white background into different tones.  GIF export plug-ins can help provide optimal dithering schemes.

**dodge:** A photographic term for blocking part of an image as it is exposed, lightening its tones.

**driver:** A software interface used to allow an applications program to communicate with a piece of hardware, such as a scanner.

**emboss:** A filter technique that makes an image appear to be raised above the surface in a 3D effect.

**export:** To transfer text or images from a document to another format, using an image editor's Save As or Export functions.

**extrude:** To create a 3D effect by adding edges to an outline shape as if it were clay pushed through a mold.

**eyedropper:**  A tool used to sample color from one part of an image so it can be used to paint or draw elsewhere.

**feather:** To fade the edges of a selection to produce a less-obtrusive transition.

**file format:** A way in which a particular application stores information on a disk.

**fill:** To cover a selected area with a solid, transparent, or gradient tone or pattern.

**filter:**  An image editor feature that changes the pixels in an image to produce blurring, sharpening, and other special effects.

**font:** Originally, a group of letters, numbers, and symbols in one size and typeface, but now often used to mean any typeface.

**gamma:** A numerical way of representing the contrast of an image's midtones.  Gamma is a method of tonal correction that takes the human eye's perception of neighboring values into account.

**gamma correction:** A method for changing the brightness, contrast, or color balance of an image by assigning new values to the gray or color tones of an image. Gamma correction can be either linear or nonlinear. Linear correction applies the same amount of change to all the tones. Nonlinear correction varies the changes tone by tone, or in highlight, midtone, and shadow areas separately to produce a more accurate or improved appearance.

**gamut:** A range of color values that can be reproduced by a particular color model or device.

**Gaussian blur:** A method of diffusing an image using a bell-shaped curve instead of blurring all pixels in the selected area uniformly.

**gray component removal:** A process in which portions of an image that have a combination of cyan, magenta, and yellow are made purer by replacing equivalent amounts of all three with black.

**gray map:** A graph that shows the relationship between the original brightness values of an image and the output values after image processing.

**grayscale:** The range of different gray values an image can have.

**guides:** Grid lines that can be used to help position objects in an image.

**halftoning:** A way of simulating the gray tones of an image by varying the size of the dots used to show the image.

**handles:** Small squares that appear in the corners and (frequently) the sides of a selection or object that can be used to resize, rotate, or otherwise manipulate the entire object or selection.

**highlight:** The brightest values in a continuous-tone image.

**histogram:** A barlike graph that shows the distribution of tones in an image.

**HSB color model:** A model that defines all possible colors by specifying a particular hue and then adding or subtracting percentages of black or white.

**hue:** A pure color.

**image map** (also called *clickable image*, or *clickable map*): A graphical image that has an associated server-side or client-side map file that lets users select links by clicking on certain portions of the image.

**inline image:** A graphic that can be viewed in the same browser window as the text, as opposed to with a separate viewing helper program.

**interlacing:** A way of displaying a GIF image in two fields: odd-numbered lines first, then even-numbered lines, thereby updating or refreshing half the image on the screen at a time, allowing visitors to view a rough version of an image even before the entire file has been downloaded from a Web page.

**interpolation:** A technique used to calculate the value of the new pixels required whenever you resize or change the resolution of an image, based on the values of surrounding pixels.

**invert:** To change an image into its negative; black becomes white, white becomes black, dark gray becomes light gray, and so forth. Colors are also changed to the complementary color; green becomes magenta, blue turns to yellow, and red is changed to cyan.

**jaggies:** The staircasing effect applied to edges of bit-mapped objects that are not perfectly horizontal or vertical.

**JPEG compression:** A method for reducing the size of an image by dividing it into blocks of varying size (depending on the amount of compression requested) and representing all the pixels in that block by a smaller number of values.

**justified:** Text aligned at both right and left margins.

**kern:** To adjust the amount of space between two adjacent letters.

**lasso:** A tool used to select irregularly-shaped areas in a bit-mapped image.

**layer:** Individual "transparent" overlays within a drawing or image file that can be edited or manipulated separately, and later composited into a single drawing or image.

**layer mask:** A grayscale mask applied only to one layer of an image.

**leading:** The amount of vertical spacing between lines of text measured from baseline to baseline.

**lens flare:** The effect used by spreading light as if it were being reflected by the internal elements of an optical lens.

**LHS color:** A system of color based on the luminance, hue, and saturation of an image.

**lighten:** An image editing function that is the equivalent to the photographic darkroom technique of dodging. Gray tones in a specific area of an image are gradually changed to lighter values.

**line art:** Usually, images that consist only of white pixels and one color.

**line screen:** The resolution or frequency of a halftone screen, expressed in lines per inch.

**lines per inch (lpi):** The method used for measuring halftone resolution.

**link:** A pointer from one position in an HTML to another position, page, or URL.

**lithography:** Offset printing.

**luminance:** The brightness or intensity of an image.

**LZW compression:** A method of compacting TIFF files using the Lempel-Zev Welch compression algorithm.

**magic wand:** A tool used to select contiguous pixels that have the same color value, or that of a range you select.

**map file:** File on the server that includes pixel coordinates of hotspots on an image map.

**mapping:** Assigning colors or grays in an image.

**marquee:** A selection tool used to mark rectangular and elliptical areas.

**mask:** To protect part of an image so it won't be affected by other operations.

**midtones:** Parts of an image with tones of an intermediate value.

**Moiré:** An objectionable pattern caused by the interference of halftone screens, frequently generated by rescanning an image that has already been halftoned.

**monochrome:** Having a single color.

**negative:** A representation of an image in which the tones are reversed. See also *invert*.

**neutral color:** In RGB mode, a color in which red, green, and blue are present in equal amounts, producing a gray.

**noise:** Random pixels added to an image to increase apparent graininess.

**opacity:** The opposite of transparency; the degree to which a layer obscures the view of the layer beneath. High opacity means low transparency.

**palette:** Tones available to produce an image, or a row of icons representing the available tools.

**pixel:** A picture element of a screen image.

**plug-In:** A filter or some other added feature, such as PhotoTools' toolbars.

**point:** Approximately 1/72 of an inch outside the Macintosh world, exactly 1/72 of an inch within it.

**Portable Network Graphics:** A new RGB file format supported by Photoshop 4.0 and, eventually, Web browsers. It offers progressive, interleaved display, more sophisticated transparency capabilities than the GIF format, but, unlike JPEG, is a lossless format.

**portrait:** The orientation of a page in which the longest dimension is vertical; also called *tall orientation*.

**posterization:** An effect produced by reducing the number of tones in an image to a level at which the tones are shown as poster-like bands.

**progressive JPEG:** A type of JPEG image in which increasingly detailed versions of an image are displayed, allowing a visitor to a Web site to view a graphic in rough form before it is completely downloaded.

**raster image:** An image defined as a set of pixels or dots in row-and-column format.

**rasterize:** The process used to convert an outline-oriented image such as an Adobe Illustrator of Corel Draw file into pixels.

**reflective copy:** Original artwork viewed by light reflected from its surface, rather than transmitted through it.

**resampling:** The process of changing the size or resolution of an image, by replacing pixels with additional pixels or fewer pixels calculated by examining the value of their neighbors.

**rescaling:** The operation of changing the dimensions of an image by reducing or enlarging the height and width in proportion to its overall dimensions.

**resolution:** The number of pixels, samples, or dots per inch in an image.

**retouch:** To edit an image, most often to remove flaws or to create a new effect.

**RGB color model:** A way of defining all possible colors as percentages of red, green, and blue.

**rubber stamp:** A Photoshop tool that copies or clones part of an image to another area or image.

**saturation:** The purity of color; the amount by which a pure color is diluted with white or gray.

**scale:** To change the size of a piece of an image.

**scanner:** A device that converts an image of reflective art or a transparency to a bit-mapped image.

**secondary color:** A color produced by mixing two primary colors, such as yellow and cyan inks to create blue, or red and green light to create magenta.

**selection:** An area of an image chosen for manipulation, usually surrounded by a moving series of dots called a selection border.

**serif:** Short strokes at the ends of letters.

**server-side image map:** A way of navigating a Web page using an image map that transfers the coordinates of the user's mouse on a Web page back to the server, where a CGI program determines which URL to direct you to.

**shade:** A color with black added.

**shadows:** The darkest part of an image holding detail.

**sharpening:** Increasing the apparent sharpness of an image by boosting the contrast between adjacent pixels that form an edge.

**smoothing:** To blur the boundaries between edges of an image, often to reduce a rough or jagged appearance.

**smudge:** A tool that smears part of an image, mixing surrounding tones together.

**snap:** A Photoshop feature that causes lines or objects being drawn or moved to be attracted to a grid or guides.

**subtractive colors:** The primary colors of pigments: cyan, magenta, and yellow used for printing.

**threshold:** A predefined level used to determine whether a pixel will be represented as black or white.

**thumbnail:** A miniature copy of a page or image that provides a preview of the original.

**TIFF(Tagged Image File Format):** A standard graphics file format that can be used to store grayscale and color images plus selection masks.

**tint:** A color with white added to it.

**tolerance:** The range of color or tonal values that will be selected (when using a tool like the magic wand) or filled with paint (when using a tool like the paint bucket).

**trim size:** Final size of a printed publication.

**undercolor removal:** A technique that reduces the amount of cyan, magenta, and yellow in black and neutral shadows by replacing them with an equivalent amount of black. See also gray component removal.

**unsharp masking:** The process for increasing the contrast between adjacent pixels in an image, increasing sharpness.

**vector image:** An image defined as a series of straight-line vectors and curves.

**W3C ( The World Wide Web Consortium):** An organization that seeks to guide standards related to the World Wide Web and that works in concert with the Internet Engineering Task Force. It is funded by contributions from a diversity of member organizations.

**web site:** A term used for the documents and resources of a particular set of Web pages.

**webmaster**. The individual responsible for managing a specific Web site.

**x-height:** The height of a lowercase letter, such as the letter x, excluding ascenders and descenders.

**zoom:** To enlarge part of an image so that it fills the screen, making it easier to work with that portion.

# About the CD

The CD-ROM packaged with this book includes tryout versions of 20 different filter packages, either as freeware (which you can use without cost), fully-functional time-limited versions (which expire after a trial period), and partially-functional demonstration software. On the CD you'll find the following files and software, all accessible to both Windows and Macintosh platforms:

- Full color versions of every figure in the book
- Image files for the color insert plates
- Working files that can be used to reproduce some of my effects
- Tryout versions of Andromeda's Series 1, Series 2, Series 3, and Shadow filters
- Tryout versions of Extensis's Intellihance, MaskPro, PhotoFrame, and PhotoTools filters
- A demonstration version of Alien Skin's Eye Candy
- A treasure trove of freeware and tryout versions of ULead's filters and applications including Art Texture, Capture, Cool 3D, Fantasy Plug-In, GIF Animator, Photo Explorer, SmartSaver, Type Plug-In, Viewer, Web Album, and Web Plug-In.

# Index